VEGETARIAN HOLIDAY FEASTS

Beth
Stun Masley

This book is dedicated to our children, Lucas and Marcos,
and to all children discovering healthy and delicious vegetarian holiday feasts.

VEGETARIAN
HOLIDAY FEASTS

STEVEN MASLEY, M.D.

Selected recipes by Nicole Vidal Masley, B.S.N.

Vitality Books, Dunedin, Florida

Cover Design by Carol Fairhurst

Text Design by Julia Hill Gignoux

Holiday Recipe Illustrations by Stéphan Daigle

Petite Mama Picking Fruit by Annouchka Galouchko, used with permission from the illustrator, from the book, *The Island of Spice*, written by Richardo Keens-Douglas

Photography by Steven Masley, M.D.   Selected photos by Kim Zumwalt.

Published by Vitality Books, Dunedin, Florida

Library of Congress Control Number 00–132661

ISBN 0-9659977-3-1

Printed in China

Contents

"Most holiday feasts are deadly when it comes to the foods they provide. Finally, Dr. Steven Masley has created a cookbook that provides festive holiday foods that not only taste delicious but are healthy for you as well. These healthier alternatives to the traditional holiday fare makes it a must cookbook for any health conscious cook."
John Westerdahl, M.P.H., R.D., C.N.S., Nutrition Editor for Veggie Life Magazine and Co-Author for The Millennium Cookbook.

"A great resource for anyone looking for the nutritional benefits of a plant-based diet. The flavors and colors of these recipes will make any meal more festive. Don't save this book just for the holidays!"
Nadine Pazder, M.S., R.D., Morton Plant Mease HealthCare and Spokesperson for the American Dietetic Association

"Holidays are a time of celebration, family, friends, and gratitude; the enjoyment of these special times is not dependent on having meat at the 'center of the plate.' **Vegetarian Holiday Feasts** will be useful and inspiring to anyone seeking healthy, delicious and easy to prepare plant-based holiday menus."
Cathy Geier, Executive Chef, Café Flora, Seattle

"Vegetarian cooking means beautiful, flavorful, healthful foods that nourish the body as well as the spirit. In Vegetarian Holiday Feasts, Dr. Steven Masley shows how easy it can be to create exciting new holiday traditions featuring simply prepared, delicious and nutritious meals that everyone will love."
*Suzanne Havala, M.S., R.D., Author of **The Natural Kitchen** and **The Complete Idiot's Guide to Being Vegetarian**, and Nutrition Advisor for the American Dietetic Association's Vegetarian Resource Group.*

"If you thought healthy holidays was an oxymoron, think again! With Dr. Masley's incredibly creative cooking, you can have your Christmas Bûche de Noël, and eat it too. This cookbook is a MUST for anyone who cares about his/her health, the health of the planet, and the welfare of animals ALL YEAR' ROUND. I can't wait for the next holiday to showcase these fabulous foods!"
John D. Borders, Jr., J.D., EarthSave International Chair, Board of Directors

"Twenty percent of all premature cancer and cardiovascular deaths are related to diet and activity level. Eating a diet low in fat and high in fruits, vegetables, and grains reduces this risk. People find it easiest to make dietary changes when they are given ideas for meals. Dr. Steven Masley has presented us with creative meals that improve our nutrition and protect us from disease. His recipes are both festive and healthy."
Beverly Green, M.D., M.P.H., Chair Committee on Prevention, Group Health Cooperative, Seattle, WA

"Vegetarian Holiday Feasts is a must for anyone wishing to prepare more healthful holiday meals without giving up flavor or pizzazz. Dr. Masley's presentations are beautiful and the aromas from these meals are seductive. Your family and guests will be impressed and amazed that food this good can be good for you. I know I'll be cooking from his book for many years to come."
Kevin J. Fichtner, Chair EarthSave Seattle

Acknowledgments

It gives me great pleasure to extend my deepest and heartfelt appreciation to all the people who have helped me to create this book. This book started shortly after writing *The 28-Day Antioxidant Diet Program,* and would not have been completed without the assistance and encouragement of many people.

My wife, Nicole, has been extremely supportive of the work involved in researching, recipe testing, and in the writing of this book. Additionally, she created several of the recipes included in this cookbook, functioned as the managing editor for Vitality Books, and created the shopping lists for each holiday.

Once again, my extended family has provided many appreciated suggestions regarding the recipes and text. They include Arpad and Peggy Masley, Evelyn and Charles Odegaard, and Joy and Jean Vidal. Several friends provided editing suggestions, in particular Pat Carlson and Julia Sokoloff.

I am grateful to the staff at two hospital libraries that have been extremely helpful in aiding my exploration and evaluation of the health benefits of the many ingredients selected in this book. At Morton Plant in Clearwater, Florida, I would like to thank Karen Roth, Tricia Whitaker and the many Morton Plant Hospital volunteers. At Providence St. Peter Hospital in Olympia, Washington, I would like to thank Edean Berglund, Kathy Wagner, and Lewis Daniell, and their helpful volunteers.

I feel fortunate to have worked in the kitchens of two wonderful restaurants in Seattle, Washington. I want to thank the staff at Café Flora, a Vegetarian Gourmet Restaurant, for welcoming me into their restaurant, especially their executive chef, Catherine Geier. I'm also grateful to the extended restaurant staff at the Four Seasons Hotel in Seattle for inviting me into an internship in their kitchen and pastry stations.

My clinical colleagues have been very supportive of my desire to pursue work apart from seeing patients in our clinic. I want to thank my former workmates at Group Health Cooperative's Olympia Medical Center in Olympia, Washington, and to my current colleagues at the Turley Family Health Center with Morton Plant Mease Health Care in Clearwater, Florida.

The modern computer era has made it much easier for people like myself to write and publish a book. I would like to thank Matt Metcalf, Steve Powers, Jean Vidal, and Craig Winters for their teaching and assistance. In particular, Jean Vidal has been very helpful as he assisted with scanning photographs and converting the text from FrameMaker® to PageMaker®. Craig Winters helped me with the design of my Web Page (www.drmasley.com), which has added a new dimension to my ability to communicate and educate worldwide.

EarthSave has been a dynamic force in my choice to make these recipes not just vegetarian, but to include vegan recipes for every holiday as well. My goal to empower people to choose food that is delicious, healthy, and is produced in an earth-friendly fashion has been strongly supported by EarthSave. Nationwide, EarthSave's staff has been supportive and friendly and I'm grateful for their help.

I also want to thank Claire Gerus, who edited my last book, *The 28-Day Antioxidant Diet Program.* She encouraged me toward clearer writing, and I'm grateful for her time and effort.

I am indebted to the many people who added an artistic touch to this book. Stéphan Daigle and Annouchka Galouchko provided ideas and painted panels to make the photographs more colorful and pleasing. Annouchka provided an illustration for the appendix, and Stéphan added the illustrations for each holiday. I also want to extend a special thanks to Lucas Masley who created two of the background panels for the photos. Selected photos were taken by Kim Zumwalt and generously given to me for this book. Michelle and Gary Crosby added background touches to several photographs, too.

I extend a special thanks to Carol Fairhurst and Julia Hill Gignoux. Carol produced the cover design and my Vitality Books company logo. Julia modified the text design for the book and produced the color patterns used for each holiday.

Lastly, I want to thank my many patients in Washington, Arizona, and Florida for their encouragement and support in creating a healthy holiday recipe plan.

Introduction

Holidays help families join together to share love and traditions. While many holiday meals focus on an entrée, such as turkey, ham, or even hamburgers, this book offers a delicious departure from meat-based menus. I've put together my favorite vegetarian holiday feasts that are fun to prepare, amazingly healthy, and leave you feeling fantastic.

Over the last few years, I've received many requests from people wanting healthy, yet delicious holiday meals. At the same time, vegetarians and vegans have asked me to create vegetarian holiday meal plans. This book was written by popular demand to meet both those needs. You will discover that every holiday has options for vegans and vegetarians, and that I have chosen healthy ingredients as the cornerstone for these recipes.

This is the first cookbook I've seen to feature healthy, meat-free meals for holidays covering all four seasons. Now you can enjoy *"Christmas Crêpes"* or *"Leek and Mushroom Soufflé"* for Christmas, a golden Nut Loaf wrapped in Fillo Dough for Thanksgiving, and an individually wrapped *"Mushroom-Pecan Paté"* pastry for an adult birthday dinner party. For desserts, consider *"Poached Pears in Hazelnut Cake,"* *"Chocolate Soufflé with Raspberry Sauce,"* or *"Chocolate Cake with Mocha Icing."*

As you prepare these recipes, your home will be fragrant as sauces simmer and the scent of herbs wafts through the kitchen. Making these recipes should be fun, as they are mostly simple to prepare, and most of the preparation can be completed before your guests arrive. I hope you will agree that while the ingredients will fill you with health and vitality, they are also incredibly satisfying. I wish you fabulous holiday feasts all year long.

Benefits of Eating Well Over the Holidays

*"My goal in creating each recipe
is to choose foods that taste delicious
and fill you with vitality."*

FEEL LIGHT WHEN YOU EAT RIGHT

To me, the best part of eating well is the resulting energy boost that comes with it. I have more fun when I choose to eat right. And, more than any other time, I want to feel energetic during the holidays.

Did you ever notice that you can't feel stuffed and vivacious at the same time? Think about how you feel after a typical meal that starts with greasy potato chips dipped in a high-fat spread. Next comes the main course: a large steak, a baked potato smothered in butter and sour cream, and bread and butter on the side. You finish the meal with a slice of pie made with flaky-buttery crust and topped with ice cream.

While that meal might appeal to some people, ten minutes after it, you would be hard-pressed to get out of your chair, let alone have fun with family or guests. If you hope to read a book to the children, go dancing, or take a walk with family–forget it!

I'll admit that when I changed my eating toward energy-enhancing foods, I initially missed feeling stuffed after a meal. I still remember a fleeting, pleasant feeling when I loaded up with high-fat, high-protein food. The problem was that any pleasure was short-lived, and for hours I couldn't get up and start going. Now, I prefer that light, satisfied feeling after a meal. I'm eating tastier foods, I'm alert, and I feel fantastic!

While food and drink take center stage at the dining table over the holidays, we also need to keep active. Exercise improves digestion and appetite, and is especially needed when facing the prospect of larger-than-usual meals. A group walk one to two hours before dining stimulates the appetite. So enjoy a walk, a hike, a bicycle ride, or plan some form of group activity.

During the holidays, dancing is one of my favorite activities. It provides a great way to have fun and spend quality time with family and friends. Pick a couple of your favorite tunes and play them between hors d'oeuvres and the first course. Dancing can improve your appetite and add fun to your holiday celebration!

SUCCEED WITH WEIGHT CONTROL OVER THE HOLIDAYS

You can eat fantastic food without gaining weight. Too often over the holidays, people gain weight and never lose it. Pinning one's hopes on a New Year's resolution to correct a 10–20 pound weight gain often leads to disappointment. The few who do lose the added weight after the holidays, often regain it over the next year. The best long-term weight-control strategy is to avoid gaining weight in the first place.

Aim to eat quality food, skipping the dips and cookies that come your way. Candies, high-fat cakes, and extra sweets are potential disasters in the making for the weight conscious. If a variety of food offerings tempts you at a party, focus on one or two items, and enjoy them "one nibble at a time." Look for fruit and vegetable dishes and skip the high-fat dips.

How can you feel satisfied while eating less food? Dine the way the French do and eat more slowly. The French and many Europeans remain slim and satisfied by enjoying leisurely meals with much smaller servings than we typically eat in the United States. They feel satisfied with smaller portions because the body feels appeased about twenty minutes after eating food. Not only will you feel more contented when you choose to eat slowly, but you'll savor the tastes and enjoy the meals more fully, too.

If you know that you usually gain weight between mid-November and early January, I strongly suggest that you increase your activity level during that period. Find a walking partner early in the season and meet regularly, preferably five to six times per week. Twenty minutes of activity three days per week is good for your health, but has not produced consistent weight control in clinical studies. A three-mile brisk walk, five to six days per week, is the best way to control your weight. If you like exercise machines, aim for a 300–400 calorie workout five to six days per week. Plan walks with friends and family, or schedule activities like skiing, dancing, or biking, especially over the winter holiday season.

Obviously, an inactive person can't reach these levels of activity all at once. It may take weeks or months to get results. For guidance, look in my book, **The 28-Day Antioxidant Diet Program,** for the fast track to exercise success. If you have health problems, always check with your medical provider before starting an exercise program.

Tips For Holiday Weight Control

- Plan to maintain your weight over the holidays
- Choose quality foods, skipping the junk
- Eat slowly. It takes twenty minutes to feel satisfied from eating
- Aim for at least a 30-minute aerobic workout 5–6 days per week

SHARE HEALTH WITH YOUR LOVED ONES

Holidays should be the best of times for families. Fortunately, a couple of days of poor eating won't change the plaque in your arteries, nor will it have an impact on your cholesterol level. However, bad food choices instantly increase your risk of strokes and heart attacks by making your blood sticky and causing your arteries to spasm. This is especially important for people with known blood vessel obstructions (those with a history of heart attacks, angina, or strokes). When people with these known health problems eat butter, fatty cheese, most margarines, or meats high in saturated fat and/or trans fats, they increase their immediate risk of "*bad events,*" heart attacks, strokes, and sudden death.

The *"good news"* is that you can eat fantastic food and enhance your health! This cookbook features healthy foods and healthy fat choices that taste great. With my recipes, you can finally have a delicious slice of cake that will be good for you, too. (See *"Chocolate Cake with Mocha Icing"* on page 122.)

In fact, even people with heart disease can eat foods containing fat during the holidays. What's important is to use fat in moderation and to choose *"healthy types of fat."* While I usually stress limiting fat to less than 20% of total calories on a day to day basis, I allow up to 30–35% of calories from fat for holiday meals.

You'll discover that I select healthy fats for my recipes–those rich in monounsaturated and omega-3 fats. These types of fats are found in olive oil, canola oil, nuts (especially almonds, hazelnuts, cashews, and macadamia nuts) avocados, and seafood. The fats in these food sources, used in moderation, can actually improve your circulation and add valuable antioxidants to your diet. For details on nutrition, see my book, *The 28-Day Antioxidant Diet Program.*

I will also add a variety of healthy foods to improve your blood circulation and your energy while enhancing the flavor of your meals. These tasty and energy-packed foods include herbs, garlic, ginger, and special fruits and vegetables that are rich in antioxidants.

IMPROVE YOUR ROMANTIC LIFE

Holidays provide a wonderful opportunity for couples to share warmth and affection. But what happens when you fill up with low-nutrient, high-fat food? You feel tired, your energy is diverted to help digest that fatty load in your stomach, and your arteries spasm, slowing vital circulation. A big steak, fatty foods, and romance just don't mix.

The best foods for romance are the same foods that enhance exercise performance–vegetables, dense grains, fruits, herbs, spices, nuts, and legumes. Not only are these foods good for your health, they are great for your energy level and they will add sizzle to your love-life!

Don't forget fluids. Hydration helps our bodies function actively. Try seltzers, herbal teas, juices, and water.

Alcohol can decrease sexual performance, especially for men. If you wish, you can enjoy one or two glasses of champagne or wine, but avoid drinking additional alcohol. Instead, drink sparkling cider, special bottled water, or your favorite herbal infusions.

Buy some flowers and light the candles! Special touches create an atmosphere that fosters love, romance, and happiness over the holiday season. Let your inner joy shine brightly during the holidays.

Romantic Dining

Special Holiday Foods

COLOR YOUR HOLIDAYS

To make your meals more festive, pick vibrant plant colors that match the holiday. Brightly colored fruits and vegetables make meals look spectacular and greatly increase your vitality. Plants produce colorful pigments (phytonutrients and antioxidants) to protect themselves from ultraviolet light. When you eat these plants, you promote your health, too.

For Thanksgiving, choose the colors of autumn (yellow, orange, red, and gold) by choosing meals made with pumpkin, squash, corn, sweet potatoes, colorful peppers and yams. Cranberry sauce provides a rich red to any table. Sliced pecans, almonds, and hazelnuts add a beautiful garnish to dishes.

For Christmas, choose greens, reds, and whites. Red and green bell peppers, tomatoes, asparagus, broccoli, kale and other greens, peas, green beans, cauliflower, and mashed potatoes create a festive table. Cranberry sauce again goes well with winter meals and adds a splash of color to the table.

For a Fourth of July Party, choose foods that are red, white, and blue. Serve "*Stars & Stripes Lasagna*" and "*Blueberry & Strawberry Crumble*" for any patriotic celebration and wait for the compliments to roll in!

Color Your Holidays

Meal Planning and Preparation

Holidays are best spent enjoying your family and friends, not slaving over a hot stove. Most of my **Vegetarian Holiday Feasts'** recipes can be prepared in advance, and assembled at the last moment. It's fun involving family and friends in the final meal preparation.

You'll find shopping lists in the appendix, so you won't find yourself missing a key ingredient at the last moment. (Make sure that essential ingredients don't disappear between shopping and serving.) I find that an ingredient search the night before saves me from *"last-minute-panic,"* especially when the house is packed with company.

Most sauces can be prepared a few days in advance and refrigerated or frozen. Involve family and friends, especially children, with advanced food preparation so that they feel part of the celebration. Cooking together provides a sense of "tradition" to special holidays that modern living has too often abandoned.

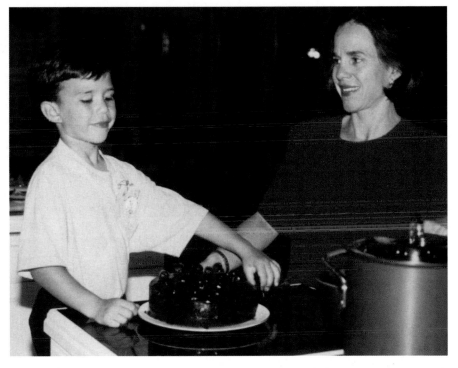

Nicole & Marcos Decorating a Cake

When my wife, Nicole, and I first married, we approached holiday cooking quite differently. I was happy to spend a holiday in the kitchen cooking, while Nicole wanted everything made in advance, so we could socialize with our guests. Over the years, we've compromised and created our own traditions for holiday meal preparation. An organized meal plan has greatly enhanced our celebrations and reduced our holiday stress.

I hope you enjoy making these delicious meals, and that preparing them increases your enjoyment with each holiday season.

Cooking Equipment and Ingredients

COOKING EQUIPMENT

You don't need an expensive kitchen to cook delicious meals. All of the recipes in this book were created with an everyday oven, common pots, pans, and utensils. However, there are several items that I find essential and others that are big time savers.

- More than any kitchen tool, I need a good knife. A high-quality knife lasts a lifetime, so go ahead and splurge at the kitchen equipment store. I prefer a chopping blade (such as a chef's knife) at least 9 inches long and 1 1/2 inches wide at the base. You'll also need a tool to keep your blade sharp.
- Use that knife on a large, solid cutting board. Especially over the holidays, I run out of cutting space on smaller cutting boards. If you use a sliding cutting board, pull it out and place it solidly on the kitchen counter. You'll cut more skillfully and safely when the cutting board doesn't wiggle.
- A collapsible metal steamer works wonders with vegetables. One steamer fits all my pots and pans. Oriental bamboo steamers are handy as they can be stacked.
- A blender can make fruit smoothies, blend soups, form sauces, and mix fruit and yogurt for frozen yogurt. The next step up is a food processor that blends the above items, cuts and slices vegetables, and grates soy or dairy cheese–thereby saving you time. If you choose recipes with beaten egg whites, a hand-held electric beater works well; fancier machines can knead bread and pizza dough, too.
- Nonstick skillets are essential. They'll help you sauté foods without using excess fats and oils. For day-to-day cooking, I rarely need a second skillet to prepare one meal. But over the holidays, I need a second skillet almost every time.
- A large stainless steel pot is great for soups, sauces, or boiling water for pasta.
- Extra measuring spoons and cups make cooking easier. They are inexpensive, so keep spares on hand. Measuring oils is easy with all the new tools to choose from, such as squirt bottles that squirt precisely 1/2 teaspoon! Many spray bottles spray 1/6 teaspoon per second–just count "one thousand one" out loud and stop. You use far less oil by spraying a thin film than you can pouring it out of the bottle.
- See-through sealable containers conveniently store food. Use short, flat ones for herbs with a splash of water to keep the herbs from spoiling. It helps to stick to 3 or 4 sizes that use the same lids so that you aren't constantly searching for matches. Plus, you can stack the same size containers to save space. Having see-through sealable containers makes it easy for guests to help assemble the ingredients. Make sure they are microwave hardy if you use them to reheat food.

I personally avoid regular aluminum pots and pans. Although the press often condemns aluminum, to date there is insufficient scientific evidence to say that cooking with aluminum is harmful. Fortunately, anodized aluminum pans offer a clear improvement over regular aluminum pans. Anodized aluminum pans usually have a nonstick surface (such as Calphalon®) and undergo an electrochemical process, making them 30% harder than stainless steel. They leak far less aluminum into food, less than you get from having an occasional cookie or piece of cake containing baking powder, and lots less than you get from taking antacids, such as Tums®.

Nonstick stainless steel and anodized aluminum make better pans that last longer, and in the long run might save you money. If scientists ever prove that regular aluminum pans are harmful, you'll be glad you switched. If aluminum pans turn out to be harmless, you will have benefited from using higher quality cooking pans.

INGREDIENTS

I have tried to limit the ingredients to those available at regular grocery stores. If I choose something that might be difficult to find, I'll also suggest an alternate ingredient.

Some of these recipes feature alcoholic beverages. When you cook or sauté with alcohol, the alcohol evaporates and all that remains is the flavor. If you wish to avoid alcohol entirely, you can either use non-alcoholic wine in place of wine, or orange extract in place of orange liqueurs. Replacing wine with non-alcoholic wine changes the flavor very little.

Fennel

Whole wheat pastry flour used to be hard to find in stores, but most large grocery stores carry it now. If you can't find whole wheat pastry flour, substitute with half whole wheat flour and half all purpose flour.

Health food stores often carry canola oil spreads without saturated fats or trans fats. Sometimes I use these spreads for pie crusts and holiday cookies in place of canola oil. Most margarines contain either trans fats or saturated fats–both are artery cloggers. If it doesn't say "No Trans Fats," the margarine likely contains these nasty ingredients. Look for Spectrum® Spread as an example of a spread without saturated fat or trans fats. Or, simply use chilled canola oil instead of margarine.

When sautéing with small amounts of oil, use spray oils rather than pouring oil as you can cover the pan better with less oil. To enhance your sautéing technique, heat your sauté pan for twenty seconds, add the oil and heat another fifteen seconds, then add the food to be sautéed. (Avoid getting distracted and burning the oil or the pan!) Most vegetables sauté better when you cook them in a pre-heated pan, promoting that *"al dente"* crunch when you chew, and sealing the flavor and nutrients in the food.

I encourage you to try different fruits, berries, beans, nuts, grains, and vegetables in place of those called for in these recipes. You can modify these recipes to fit either your tastes or preferences, or to use what you can find and afford in your local grocery store.

I pick flavorful, health-promoting mushrooms for many recipes, but you can substitute regular button mushrooms if you wish. Nutritionally, fresh shiitake and oyster mushrooms are better. Dried shiitakes, soaked in water 20–30 minutes, work well in most recipes; look for them at a bargain price in Oriental food stores. Other dried wild mushrooms are also good substitutes. While button mushrooms are cheaper, they contain far less flavor and they lack the known health-promoting aspects of many Oriental mushrooms.

You will discover that I use leeks in many of my recipes. Leeks have a milder flavor than onions, and seem to produce less gas or bad breath for people who are sensitive to eating onions. Also, leeks are rich in antioxidants and phytonutrients. If you have trouble finding leeks, you can substitute one-half medium onion for one leek in a recipe, or use one third cup of chopped green onions.

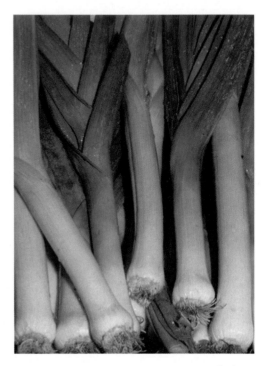

Leeks

I use fennel in many recipes. Fennel has a lovely anise flavor, and it is packed with antioxidant nutrients. It is commonly used in Mediterranean cuisine.

I enjoy using miso paste in vegetable stock, soups, and gravy. Miso is a brown paste made from soybeans with a soy sauce flavor. It provides a bold, earthy taste in dishes, and provides valuable nutrients. Miso is loaded with salt. So, if you are salt-sensitive, substitute low-salt vegetable stock cubes or cut the miso serving size in half. Look for miso in the produce section near the tofu in your grocery store. If you don't see it quickly, ask. Many times, the first grocery store staff helper I asked couldn't find it, but the second person could. If it's not available, you can use one tablespoon of low-sodium soy sauce for each tablespoon of miso paste. Miso stores well for months in the refrigerator.

Sea vegetables (seaweeds) are highly nutritious and add a rich flavor to soups, salads and sautés. For the sushi recipe for New Year's Eve, look for sheets of nori. If the nori sheets haven't been toasted, hold each sheet over a hot burner or gas flame for a minute. If you don't find nori sheets, toasted wakame sheets have a savory flavor, too. If your local grocery store doesn't carry sheets of seaweed, visit an Oriental food store.

Seitan, also called braised wheat gluten, has a nice chewy texture and marinates beautifully. It brings a wonderful texture to many stir-fry dishes and Mexican food. I've included it in the New Year's Eve and Cinco de Mayo dinner menus. Ask for it in Oriental food stores.

A healthy, delicious holiday dessert can include *"fine chocolate."* Quality chocolate is made with cocoa powder, cocoa butter, plus vanilla, sugar, and lecithin. Skip all the cheap chocolates that include milk chocolate, palm oils, and chocolate fat substitutes. These cheap cocoa butter substitutes ruin the rich chocolate flavor. They also are also bad for your health.

Fine chocolate with pure cocoa butter contains healthy fats. It also provides a rich source of magnesium and many chemical compounds that help people manage stress–who couldn't use help handling stress over the holidays? Quality chocolate is high in calories and fat content, so I use it in moderation. Enjoy drizzling it over desserts, or offer a small chocolate treat on the side of a dessert plate.

VEGETARIAN OR VEGAN

By definition, vegetarians eat foods that are produced, including all plant foods and dairy products such as cow's milk, cheese, and eggs. They don't eat fish, shellfish, poultry, or any other meat. Vegans only eat plant foods, and do not eat dairy products or eggs.

My goal for this book is to provide holiday meals for both vegetarians and vegans. You can use non-fat cow's milk or soy milk. As soy milk tends to be thicker than cow's milk, some recipes will call for an extra quarter cup of water per cup of milk to yield the right consistency. In several recipes, you could also use rice milk in place of cow's milk. From a health perspective, calcium-fortified soy milk is the healthiest form of milk, as it contains calcium, plus a vast variety of phytonutrients, anti-aging and antioxidant compounds, and beneficial plant hormones.

Some holidays will give you the choice between a vegetarian or vegan main course or dessert. For example, Christmas Eve offers either a *"Leek & Mushroom Soufflé"* (includes egg whites) or a *"Butternut Squash and Spinach Risotto"* for the main course (vegan). The "Cinco de Mayo" holiday gives you the choice of *"Sweet Potato Flan"* (with egg whites) or *"Fried Plantains with Banana Ice"* (vegan).

If you choose to use cow's milk or eggs, I highly encourage you to choose organic dairy products and organic, cage-free eggs. They are much better for your health, and better for the planet, too. Especially over the holiday season, be good to yourself, your family, and the Earth.

To the Holidays—Good Health, Healthy Planet, and Bon Appétit!

Thanksgiving

Thanksgiving gives us the opportunity to offer our gratitude for the incredible foods, goods, and provisions that we enjoy all year long. It is one of the few times when the meal epitomizes the holiday itself.

Having made numerous volunteer trips to rural developing countries (such as Guatemala, Kenya, Ecuador, and Pakistan) I'm thankful for all I have: running water I can drink, electricity at the flick of a finger, cooking appliances, grocery stores with endless variety, and most importantly, a healthy family. I don't just say "thank you" for the delicious Thanksgiving feast before me, but for the incredible bounty in my life.

One nice thing about Thanksgiving is that guests often linger all day, both before and after the meal. A substantial appetizer can carry you through those hours before the main feast, without ruining your appetite. The artistic *"Roasted Pepper Terrine"* fills that function nicely.

Dinner calls for a showcase main entrée and several side dishes. A large, golden nut loaf, wrapped and decorated in fillo dough and surrounded by the usual Thanksgiving trimmings provides a beautiful feast. I enjoy a light red wine (such as a fine Pinot Noir variety) or champagne, and sparkling cider with this meal. Tea goes well with dessert.

The following menu provides a lovely Thanksgiving feast for friends and family. I usually do half of the food preparation the evening before and half on Thanksgiving morning. That leaves me with most of the afternoon and evening to enjoy the holiday. I take pleasure involving guests in the final assembly of dinner since the final touches for the recipes are fun, easy, and not too messy.

Thanksgiving Dinner Menu

Roasted Pepper Terrine

✣

Nut Roast Wrapped in Fillo Dough

✣

Butternut Squash Stuffed with Grains, Pecans & Berries

✣

Mashed Potatoes with Vegetarian Gravy
Cranberry Sauce with Orange & Blueberries

✣

Apple-Pecan Pie
&
Cherry Sorbet

Thanksgiving Dinner Preparation Plan

When I invite guests to a Thanksgiving dinner celebration, I often ask them to bring comfortable shoes as we will play dancing music between courses. Schedule 5 hours to prepare this meal. For a shopping list, see page 140.

1–2 DAYS BEFORE THANKSGIVING (3 HOURS PREP TIME)
- Make gravy.
- Make nut roast filling.
- Make cranberry sauce.
- Bake squash.
- Make terrine.
- Make squash filling (keep nuts separate from rice-vegetable filling).
- Make pie crusts and assemble into pie plate. Do not bake. Refrigerate or freeze.
- Make cherry sorbet.

THANKSGIVING MORNING
- Assemble and bake pies.
- Peel potatoes, cut in 1–2 inch cubes, and cover with water in a sauce pan.

2 HOURS BEFORE THE GUESTS ARRIVE
- Assemble nut roast. Cover in plastic wrap and refrigerate.
- Sauté garlic and herbs for mashed potatoes and set aside.
- Stuff the squash and prepare garnishes.

40 MINUTES BEFORE SERVING DINNER
- Open red wine to breathe.
- Preheat oven to 375°F.

20 MINUTES BEFORE SERVING DINNER
- Bring water to a boil for the potatoes.
- Place the nut roast and stuffed squash in the oven.
- Simmer gravy, add extra stock if too thick.

10 MINUTES BEFORE SERVING DINNER
- Finish preparing mashed potatoes.
- Heat remaining squash filling.

WHEN SERVING
- Spoon potatoes on a serving dish, or pipe them onto individual plates with a piping bag.
- Place the stuffed squash on a serving platter and garnish. Put remaining squash filling in a serving dish, or serve on plates under squash.
- Transfer nut roast to a serving platter. Garnish.
- Put gravy in a serving dish.

Slice of Nut Roast

Roasted Pepper Terrine

Roasted Pepper Terrine

This colorful appetizer is Nicole's recipe. It is great on toasted pumpernickel bread or your favorite cracker. It will satisfy your guests for hours.

PREPARATION TIME: 40 MINUTES
REFRIGERATION TIME: 2 HOURS
SERVES: 10–12

Baked Tofu:

10 oz	Tofu, firm
1 medium	Garlic clove, minced
1 Tbsp	Chili powder
1 tsp	Cumin powder
1 tsp	Cumin seed
2 Tbsp	Soy sauce, low sodium
1/4 tsp	Sea salt
4 Tbsp	Rice vinegar

Pesto:

1 Tbsp	Extra virgin olive oil
1/4 cup	Walnuts
4 medium	Garlic cloves, minced
1/2 tsp	Sea salt
4 cups	Cilantro, fresh

Layers:

15 oz	Black beans, cooked and well drained
4 large	Orange bell peppers, roasted, peeled (see page 138)

Garnish:

Few	Cilantro sprigs

Preheat oven to 400°F.

Rinse and drain tofu. Pat dry with paper towels. Cut tofu into slices about 1/2-inch thick and lay them out on a nonstick baking dish. Combine the remaining tofu ingredients. Spoon 1/2 of this mixture evenly over the tofu. Bake for 10 minutes, then take out of the oven and turn the tofu slices over. Spoon remaining mixture over the other side of the tofu and bake in the oven for another 10 minutes. Remove from the oven and set aside.

Heat a skillet then add oil. Lightly toast the walnuts, garlic and salt. In a food processor or blender, combine pesto ingredients and process until finely chopped. Place pesto in a dish and set aside. Do not rinse the processor or blade. In the same container, process beans into a chunky paste.

Line a 9x4-inch loaf pan with parchment paper so that the paper covers the bottom and long sides of the pan. Slice the roasted peppers in half, lay them flat, and cover the bottom of the pan with 1/2 of the best peppers. Spread the pesto over the peppers along the bottom of the pan, patting down to an even layer. Layer the tofu over the pesto, covering it evenly. Spread the processed beans over tofu. Lay remaining peppers flat over the bean layer. Cover with plastic wrap and place three 15-ounce cans on terrine to weigh it down. Refrigerate for at least 2 hours.

Before serving, drain out any liquid that appears along the sides, remove cans and plastic wrap and invert onto a platter. Peel off parchment paper. Garnish with sprigs of cilantro. Serve with toasted pumpernickel bread or your favorite cracker.

Per Serving	Calories: 177	% Fat Calories: 31%
	Saturated Fat: 0.7 grams	Fiber: 6.8 grams
	Total Fat: 6.7 grams	Sodium: 364 mg

Nut Roast Wrapped in Fillo Dough

This dish is a lovely centerpiece for a holiday meal. Serve with mashed potatoes, gravy, cranberry sauce, and stuffed squash for a special dinner. Serve with a red wine like pinot noir, or sparkling cider.

PREPARATION TIME: 50 MINUTES
BAKING TIME: 30 MINUTES
SERVES: 10–12 (MAKES 2 NUT ROASTS)

Filling:

1 tsp	Virgin olive oil
1 medium	Leek, white only, chopped
3 medium	Carrots, diced finely
2 cups	Shiitake mushrooms, chopped
1/4 tsp	Sea salt
1 tsp	Italian herbs, dried
3/4 cup	Vegetable stock (divided)
6 medium	Garlic cloves, minced
2 Tbsp	Whole wheat pastry flour
1/2 cup	Red wine
15 oz	Stewed tomatoes, canned
1 tsp	Soy sauce, low-sodium
1 Tbsp	Miso paste

Nut mixture:

7 large	Egg whites (or 6 oz firm tofu)
2 cups	Whole wheat bread crumbs
1/2 cup	Almonds, roasted, chopped finely
1/2 cup	Cashews, roasted, chopped
12 sheets	Fillo dough (12x17-inch sheets)
	Olive oil spray

Garnish:

1/4 cup	Parsley, finely chopped
1/4 cup	Dried cranberries

Preheat oven to 375°F.

Heat a skillet over medium-high heat and add oil. Add leeks and stir, 1–2 minutes. Sauté carrots, shiitakes, salt and herbs for 2–3 minutes. Add 1/4 cup of stock and garlic. Cook 2 minutes. Add flour, stir, and heat 2 minutes. Add red wine, stewed tomatoes, and soy sauce. Simmer for 5 more minutes.

Dissolve miso in remaining 1/2 cup broth. Add to the vegetables. Reduce heat to medium low and cook another 5–10 minutes, until thick but not dry. Set aside to cool.

Beat egg whites until they form soft peaks. Fold bread crumbs and nuts into egg whites. Fold into cooled filling.

Spray 2 cookie sheets with olive oil spray. Stack 6 fillo sheets per tray spraying each sheet for 2 seconds with olive oil.

Pour half of the above mixture into the center of each stack of fillo sheets, leaving a 3-inch, filling-free fillo border. Enclose filling loosely with fillo edges, sides first then the ends. Spray each fillo roll top with virgin olive oil for 1–2 seconds.

Bake about 20 minutes, until shell is golden. Slide onto a platter and garnish with parsley and cranberries.

Vegan Option:
Replace egg whites with 6 ounces firm tofu. Purée tofu in the blender. Stir tofu into sauté mixture, adding bread crumbs and nuts. Wrap with fillo as above.

Per Serving	Calories: 384	% Fat Calories: 33%
	Saturated Fat: 2.2 grams	Fiber: 5.5 grams
	Total Fat: 14.1 grams	Sodium: 599 mg.

Butternut Squash Stuffed with Grains, Pecans & Berries

PREPARATION TIME: 30 MINUTES
BAKING AND COOKING TIME: 1 HOUR
SERVES: 10–12

1/2 cup	**Wild rice**
2 1/2 cups	**Water**
1/2 cup	**Quinoa**
1 cup	**Water**
3 medium	**Butternut squashes**
1 Tbsp	**Virgin olive oil**
1 medium	**Leek, diced (white part and first inch of light green)**
1 cup	**Shiitake mushrooms, sliced**
1 tsp	**Italian herbs, dried**
1/2 tsp	**Sea salt**
2 cups	**Broccoli flowerets, sliced**
1/2 cup	**Pecans, roasted and chopped**
2 medium	**Tomatoes, chopped**
1/2 cup	**Cranberries, frozen**

Garnish:

Few	**Parsley sprigs**
2 Tbsp	**Cranberries, dried**
2 Tbsp	**Almonds, sliced**
1 medium	**Orange, sliced**

Preheat oven to 350°F.

Bring water to a boil, add wild rice. Simmer 45–55 minutes, until al dente. Drain and set aside. Rinse quinoa, bring water to a boil. Add quinoa and simmer 15–20 minutes, until tender but still firm. Set aside.

Meanwhile, cut squash in half lengthwise and scoop out seeds and stringy pulp. Place in the oven, cut side down, on an oven pan with sides and bake for 30–40 minutes. (Don't overcook.) Scoop out a depression for the stuffing and set aside to cool.

Heat a skillet over medium heat and add oil. Add leek and mushrooms, sauté 3–4 minutes. Add herbs, salt, and broccoli. Cover, simmer 3–4 minutes, until the broccoli is tender, but still chewy. Roast pecans in microwave for 1 minute or in the oven at 350°F for 5–6 minutes. Combine pecans, tomatoes, and cranberries with sautéed vegetables and set aside.

Mix rice and quinoa with the vegetable filling and spoon into halved squash. Bake for 10–15 minutes.

To serve, place squash on a bed of the remaining warmed rice mixture. Garnish with parsley sprigs, cranberries, almond slices, and orange slices.

Per Serving	Calories: 287	% Fat Calories: 22%
	Saturated Fat: 0.8 grams	Fiber: 4.6 grams
	Total Fat: 7.6 grams	Sodium: 125 mg

Butternut Squash with Grains, Pecans & Berries

Thanksgiving Dinner

9

Mashed Potatoes with Vegetarian Gravy

This is a fluffy, low-fat version of the typically heavy holiday mashed potato dish. The garlic and herbs add a mouthwatering flavor that goes well with the gravy.

PREPARATION TIME: 20 MINUTES
SERVES: 10–12

6 medium	**Russet potatoes**
1 1/2 Tbsp	**Virgin olive oil**
6 medium	**Garlic cloves, minced**
2 tsp	**Italian herbs, dried**
1 1/2 cups	**Nonfat milk or soy milk, warmed**
1 tsp	**Sea salt**
1/4 tsp	**Ground pepper**
1/2 cup	**Fresh parsley, chopped finely**

Peel and quarter potatoes, cover with water in a pot, bring to a boil, and simmer until soft, then drain. (Save the liquid for stock if desired.) Mash potatoes in a mixer or by hand.

Heat a skillet over medium heat and add oil. Add garlic and herbs. Sauté for 1–2 minutes, until garlic is yellow but not browned.

Warm milk over low heat. Add sautéed garlic, fresh herbs, milk, salt, and pepper to potatoes and mix well. Spoon or pipe* (with a piping bag) potatoes onto individual plates, or serve in a bowl. Serve with gravy (next page).

Per Serving (incl. gravy)	Calories: 150	% Fat Calories: 20%
	Saturated Fat: 0.5 grams	Fiber: 2.9 grams
	Total Fat: 3.2 grams	Sodium: 745 mg

*Piping refers to using an icing bag to squeeze mashed food or icing into an artistic design. Try using an icing bag with different shaped nozzles to decorate your dinner plate with mashed potatoes or whipped yams. With time, you'll have fun piping food onto your guests' plates.

Don't use the same icing bag for dessert icing and dinner foods containing garlic and onion, as the onions will flavor your dessert icing. I prefer a large bag for serving mashed potatoes, and a smaller one for desserts.

Vegetarian Gravy

PREPARATION TIME: 15 MINUTES
SIMMERING TIME: 10–20 MINUTES
SERVES: 10–12

1	tsp	Virgin olive oil
2	medium	Onions, minced
4	cups	Mushrooms, minced
1/2	tsp	Sea salt
6	Tbsp	Whole wheat pastry flour
1	cup	Red wine
1	Tbsp	Soy sauce, low-sodium
1	Tbsp	Miso paste
2	cups	Vegetable stock

Heat a skillet over medium heat and add oil. Add onions, mushrooms, and salt. Stir until onions are soft and golden. Add flour and heat 2 minutes, stirring occasionally. Add red wine and soy sauce. Dissolve miso in stock. Add to above and heat until mixture thickens. In a blender, purée mixture until smooth.

Serve immediately, or store in the refrigerator or freezer. Add extra stock if the gravy becomes too thick.

Cranberry Sauce with Orange & Blueberries

This is a colorful, flavorful, holiday sauce. Serve as a side dish, or pour over baked squash. You can make it 1–2 days in advance. Refrigerate until ready to use.

PREPARATION TIME: 10 MINUTES
SIMMERING TIME: 10 MINUTES
SERVES: 10 (MAKES 3 CUPS)

1 cup		Orange juice
1/2 cup		Sugar
12 oz		Cranberries, frozen
1 medium		Orange, peeled, cut in half and chopped
1 cup		Blueberries, frozen
Garnish:		
1 Tbsp		Fresh mint leaves

Heat juice and sugar in a saucepan. When gently bubbling, add cranberries, and orange. Simmer 5 minutes. Add blueberries and simmer another 3–5 minutes until cranberries open and the sauce thickens. Remove from heat.

Serve warm or chilled. It stores well for several days covered. Garnish with mint leaves.

Per Serving	Calories: 81	% Fat Calories: 2.5%
	Saturated Fat: 0 grams	Fiber: 2.2 grams
	Total fat: 0.3 grams	Sodium: 1 mg

Apple-Pecan Pie

Enjoy this pie anytime of year. The dried cherries add a splash of color and a special flavor to the apple-pecan pie.

PREPARATION TIME: 1 HOUR
PIE DOUGH CHILLING TIME: 1–24 HOURS
BAKING TIME: 35–45 MINUTES
SERVES: 8 (ONE 9-INCH PIE)

Crust:

1 1/4 cups	Whole wheat pastry flour
3/4 cup	All purpose flour
1/2 tsp	Sea salt
1/2 cup	Canola oil, chilled
5-6 Tbsp	Water, ice cold
1/4 tsp	Sugar
1/8 tsp	Cinnamon

Filling:

2 tsp	Corn starch
1 Tbsp	Lemon juice
6 cups	Green apples, cored, peeled, and sliced
2/3 cup	Dried cherries
1/3 cup	Pecans, chopped
1/8 tsp	Nutmeg, freshly ground
2/3 cup	Brown sugar

Garnish:

Few	Sprigs of fresh mint

Preheat oven to 400°F.

Crust:

In a bowl, combine flours and salt. Blend in chilled canola oil with a fork or pastry blender until it has the consistency of cornmeal with pea sized lumps. (You can refrigerate or freeze canola oil in advance.) Handle gently, and don't over mix or the dough becomes tough. Sprinkle dough with water, one tablespoon at a time, adding just enough water to form dough into a ball. Wrap and refrigerate 1–24 hours.

Bring dough to room temperature (30–45 minutes) before rolling. Save 1/4 dough for latticed pie cover. Between wax paper or wrap, roll dough into a flat circle. Roll from center out until it's 1/8-inch thick and 2 inches wider than pie plate. Patch tears, but don't re-roll dough if possible. Spray pan lightly with canola oil. Ease dough into a 9-inch pie dish. Trim border and pinch edges. To pre-bake the pie crust, place a piece of tin foil over the pie dish and fill it with 2 cups of dried beans (or pie weights), bake 10–15 minutes. Remove the beans and foil and set aside to cool.

Filling:

Dissolve corn starch in lemon juice. Combine remaining pie filling ingredients. Add corn starch and mix well. Pour into pie shell. Roll out remaining dough, cut into 1/2-inch strips, for lattice cover. Sprinkle strips with sugar and cinnamon. Cover pie with dough strips, forming a lattice. Bake at 400°F for 10 minutes, reduce heat to 350°F for another 25–35 minutes, until crust is golden.

Serve with nonfat cherry sorbet. Garnish with fresh mint sprigs.

Per Serving	Calories: 564	% Fat Calories: 27%
(incl. sorbet)	Saturated Fat: 1.4 grams	Fiber: 63 grams
	Total Fat: 18 grams	Sodium: 145 mg

Apple-Pecan Pie (photo by Kim Zumwalt)

Cherry Sorbet

This is one of my favorite sorbet recipes, easy-to-make, healthy ingredients, and fabulous.

PREPARATION TIME: 5–10 MINUTES
FREEZING TIME: 10–15 MINUTES WITH AN ICE CREAM MAKER/6–10 HOURS IN THE FREEZER
SERVES: 8

2 cups	Orange juice
1/3 cup	Sugar
3 Tbsp	Port wine
4 cups	Cherries, frozen

Garnish:

2 tsp	Lime rind, grated
Few	Sprigs mint

In a blender purée orange juice, sugar, port, and cherries.

Freeze in an ice cream maker just before serving. Or put in a bowl in the freezer for 6 hours (it becomes too hard to serve without partially thawing after 24 hours). Optionally, add 2 tablespoons of almond oil for smoothness.

Garnish each bowl with grated lime rind and a mint leaf. Serve with apple-pecan pie, or enjoy the sorbet by itself.

Per serving

Calories: 105	% Fat Calories: 4%
Saturated Fat: 0 grams	Fiber: 1.1 grams
Total Fat: 0.5 grams	Sodium: 2 mg

Christmas

My family loves celebrating Christmas. Despite it being one of the busiest times of the year, we celebrate! Family and friends gather in our home and we participate in our local church services, including cooking for potluck dinners and caroling. We decorate a tree with lights and ornaments, put up wreaths, set out candles, and create a nativity scene. The children love putting up lights inside and outside the house.

Christmas transforms winter. Houses and stores are aglow with color. Northern towns and cities are filled with hustle and bustle, despite the cold, dark, and wet of colder climates. Even in sunny Southern states, you will find houses, palm trees, and shrubs glittering with lights.

Let the Christmas season transform you! Embrace the following delicious, healthy foods. Share warmth and kindness freely. Feel the energy of this merry holiday and let your inner light shine brightly.

Christmas Eve Dinner Menu

We enjoy this meal either before, or after celebrating with a candle-lighting ceremony at church. You can serve the soufflé plus wild rice and quinoa, or for a vegan option, serve butternut squash and spinach risotto.

Roasted Garlic Soup with Kale

✛

Leek & Mushroom Soufflé
with
Wild Rice, Quinoa & Herbs

Or

Butternut Squash & Spinach Risotto

✛

Sautéed Fennel, Red Bell Peppers & Scallions
Cranberry Sauce with Ginger & Orange

✛

Poached Pears in Hazelnut Cake

Christmas Eve Dinner Preparation Plan

I prefer to have my evening free for family, doing most of the prep work in advance. If Christmas Eve is a work day, I'll do most of the preparation 1–2 days in advance. If it is a weekend, or a holiday, I'll plan on 4 hours that same day to do all the preparations. I enjoy involving my guests in the final assembly. For a shopping list, see page 140.

1–2 DAYS BEFORE CHRISTMAS EVE DINNER (2 HOURS PREP TIME)
- Make or buy vegetable stock.
- Make garlic soup. Do not add kale.
- Make leek and shiitake white sauce for soufflé filling.
- Make cranberry sauce.
- Cook wild rice and quinoa grains.
- Prepare apricot sauce for cake.
- Prepare apple cider, seal, and store.

After you prepare these items, seal them separately in appropriate containers and store in the refrigerator.

CHRISTMAS EVE DINNER PREP (1 1/2 HOURS PREP TIME)
- Peel, prep, and simmer pears in cider. Bake pear cakes.
- Separate egg whites for the soufflé.
- Slice kale for soup.
- Prep vegetables for fennel dish.

40 MINUTES BEFORE SERVING CHRISTMAS EVE DINNER
- Sauté onions for wild rice dish, combine with quinoa and wild rice. Set aside.
- Preheat oven to 375°F.
- Beat egg whites for soufflé.
- Warm soup, and add sliced kale.

30 MINUTES BEFORE SERVING CHRISTMAS EVE DINNER
- Assemble soufflé and place in the oven.
- Enjoy soup while the soufflé bakes.

10 MINUTES BEFORE SERVING CHRISTMAS EVE DINNER
- Re-heat wild rice and quinoa dish.
- Sauté fennel dish.

WHEN SERVING DINNER
- Place cranberry sauce on the table.
- Spoon wild rice and quinoa on a serving platter, then garnish and serve.
- Spoon fennel, red bell pepper, and scallion dish on a serving plate and serve.
- Remove soufflé from the oven and serve immediately. It will collapse as it cools or is cut.

Christmas

Roasted Garlic Soup with Kale

Don't be alarmed by the quantity of garlic used here. Roasting renders the garlic mild, producing a rich soup. The kale provides a swirling, elegant shape and a contrast in color, taste, and texture. Use cabbage or spinach if you can't find kale. You can make the vegetable stock from scratch, use vegetable broth cubes with low-sodium content, or use canned vegetable broth.

PREPARATION TIME: 20–25 MINUTES
BAKING TIME: 25 MINUTES
SIMMERING TIME: 30 MINUTES
SERVES: 6

3 medium	Heads of garlic
2 pinches	Saffron (or 1/4 teaspoon Italian herbs, dried)
6 cups	Vegetable stock (see page 139)
1 tsp	Virgin olive oil
1 cup	Mushrooms, thinly sliced
3 cups	Kale, cut in 2-inch long strips (purple or green)
	Olive oil spray

Preheat the oven to 375°F.

Cut off the tops from heads of garlic, exposing the tip of each garlic clove. Spray olive oil over the cut surface. Place cut end down on a baking dish or in a muffin pan. Roast for 25 minutes in the preheated oven. If you use the muffin pan, add 1 teaspoon of water to the bottom of each muffin depression to add steam. Remove from oven. Set aside to cool. Peel or squeeze the cloves out of their shell.

Place peeled, roasted garlic cloves, saffron and vegetable stock in a blender or food processor and purée.

Heat a stockpot over medium heat and add oil. Sauté mushrooms for 3–4 minutes. Add purée to pot. Simmer for 30 minutes, allowing the flavors to combine. Add chopped kale to soup 4 minutes before serving.

Serve immediately, or refrigerate up to 2 days. Serve with warm, dense, whole-grain bread if desired.

Per Serving	Calories: 102	% Fat Calories: 19%
	Saturated Fat: 0.3 grams	Fiber: 2.4 grams
	Total Fat: 2.0 grams	Sodium: 127 mg

Garlic

Leek & Mushroom Soufflé

Soufflés add splendor to a holiday meal. They are easy and fun to make. If you've never made one, bake a practice soufflé in advance. I like the leek-shiitake flavors, but you can enjoy other wild mushroom flavors, too. Prepare the sauté and white sauce in advance. To assemble, whip the egg whites, fold with the sauté, and pop into the oven.

PREPARATION TIME: 40 MINUTES
BAKING TIME: 40 MINUTES
SERVES: 6

White sauce:

2 Tbsp	Virgin olive oil
2 medium	Leeks, sliced and chopped finely (use only the white base and the first inch of light green)
2 cups	Shiitake mushrooms, diced finely
1/2 tsp	Sea salt
1 tsp	Italian herbs, dried
5 medium	Garlic cloves, minced
1/4 cup	Whole wheat pastry flour
1 cup	Nonfat milk (or soy milk)
2 Tbsp	Parsley, finely chopped
1/2 cup	Nonfat mozzarella cheese, grated (or soy cheese)
4 Tbsp	Parmesan cheese, grated (or soy cheese)
1/4 cup	Vegetable stock (See page 139)
10 large	Egg whites
1/2 cup	Whole wheat bread crumbs

Garnish:

1 Tbsp	Almond slivers
1/4 cup	Parsley, finely chopped
1 Tbsp	Parmesan cheese, grated (optional)

Preheat oven to 375°F.

White sauce:
Heat a skillet over medium-high heat and add oil. Sauté leeks, mushrooms, salt and herbs for 2 minutes. Stir occasionally. Reduce heat to medium. Stir in garlic and flour. Continue to heat 2 minutes. Add 1/2 cup milk, stir for 2 minutes. Add remaining milk and parsley, stir, and remove from heat when thick but not dry. Set aside to cool. Add grated cheese. Stir in 2–4 tablespoons of vegetable stock to keep moist but not too wet.

Beat egg whites until stiff. Fold bread crumbs into egg whites. Gently fold white sauce into whipped egg whites. Don't over mix or you lose air and the soufflé rises poorly.

Spray a round soufflé dish (9-inch diameter, 4-inch deep) with virgin olive oil for 2–3 seconds. Pour soufflé mixture into dish. Garnish top with almond slivers, parsley, and parmesan cheese.

Bake until a knife or a long toothpick comes out clean and top is golden, 35–40 minutes. Serve immediately. The soufflé collapses when cut, or as it cools.

Per Serving	Calories: 243	% Fat Calories: 25%
	Saturated Fat: 1.5 grams	Fiber: 4.6 grams
	Total Fat: 7.2 grams	Sodium: 274 mg

Wild Rice, Quinoa & Herbs

This is a lovely, flavorful side dish. It's packed with nutrients, minerals, and antioxidants–filling you with vitality! Make extra, and store leftovers in the refrigerator or the freezer. Serve warm or chilled.

PREPARATION TIME: 15 MINUTES
COOKING TIME: 45–55 MINUTES
SERVES: 6

1 cup	**Wild rice**
4 cups	**Water**
1 cup	**Quinoa**
1 1/4 cups	**Hot water**
1/2 Tbsp	**Miso paste**
1 tsp	**Virgin olive oil**
1 medium	**Red onion, sliced thinly**
1/4 tsp	**Sea salt**
1 tsp	**Italian herbs, dried**
1/4 cup	**Vegetable stock (See page 139)**
1 cup	**Parsley, chopped finely**
3 medium	**Scallions, chopped**

Garnish:

2 Tbsp	**Almond slivers**
Few	**Parsley sprigs**

In a sauce pan, bring wild rice and water to a boil. Reduce heat, and simmer for about 50 minutes, until tender but still chewy. Strain rice and set aside.

Place quinoa in a fine strainer and rinse with water. In a sauce pan, bring water to a boil. Add rinsed quinoa. Reduce heat, stir in miso, and simmer 20 minutes. Remove from heat. Set aside.

Heat a sauté pan over medium heat and add oil. Add onion, salt, herbs, and sauté 2 minutes. Add stock, steam a few seconds. Stir in cooked rice and quinoa, parsley, and scallions. Simmer covered 2–3 minutes, stirring occasionally.

Serve warm or chilled. Garnish with almond slivers and parsley sprigs.

Per Serving	Calories: 276	% Fat Calories: 16%
	Saturated Fat: 0.5 grams	Fiber: 5.5 grams
	Total Fat: 5.0 grams	Sodium: 252 mg

Butternut Squash & Spinach Risotto

As an alternative to the soufflé and grain dish, try this fragrant risotto dish.

PREPARATION TIME: 1 HOUR
SERVES: 6

2 cups	Baby yellow squash
1 tsp	Italian herbs, dried
1/4 cup	Pecans, chopped
2 cups	Water
1 large	Butternut squash, peeled and cut into 1/2-inch cubes
2 Tbsp	Virgin olive oil
1 medium	Onion, diced
1/4 tsp	Sea salt
1/8 tsp	Ground black pepper
2 cups	Arborio rice
6 cups	Vegetable stock (See page 139)
8 cups	Fresh spinach leaves
1/4 cup	White wine (or vegetable stock)
1/4 cup	Fresh herbs (parsley and/or basil), chopped

Preheat oven to 375°F.

Spray an oven pan lightly with virgin olive oil. Cut baby squash in half and mix with herbs. Bake for 30 minutes, until tender but not too soft. Set aside to cool.

With the heated oven, bake pecans on a cookie sheet for 5 minutes. Set aside.

Bring 2 cups water to a boil. Add cubed butternut squash to boiling water for 5–10 minutes, until squash is tender but not mushy. Drain the squash, reserving the cooking water. Add cooking water to vegetable stock. Rinse squash under cold water in a colander to arrest cooking. Set aside.

Heat a sauté pan over medium-high heat and add oil. Add onion and sauté until golden. Add salt, pepper and rice. Sauté 2–3 minutes, stirring frequently. Add vegetable stock, 1 cup at a time, stirring almost constantly. As the rice thickens and is nearly dry, add another cup of stock. Continue to add stock as rice thickens. When the rice is tender but still slightly chewy, it is done. Remove from heat and cover.

Heat a sauté pan sprayed with virgin olive oil. Sauté butternut and yellow squash for 2–3 minutes over medium-high heat. Add spinach and wine. Steam about 2 minutes, until spinach is tender but not over cooked. Remove from heat. Spoon risotto on to a serving plate. Spoon squash and spinach over risotto. Garnish with herbs.

To prepare in advance, cook squash and heat risotto until 3/4 cooked. Spread risotto on a cookie sheet, and refrigerate, covered, until ready to finalize the cooking process. Reheat with 1–2 cups of stock. Sauté squash and spinach as above.

Per Serving		
	Calories: 593	% Fat Calories: 20%
	Saturated Fat: 2.1 grams	Fiber: 7.8 grams
	Total Fat: 13.2 grams	Sodium: 640 mg

Cranberry Sauce with Ginger & Orange

This is a vibrant holiday sauce, used as a side dish. You can make it several days in advance and keep stored in the refrigerator. I usually make a double batch for the holidays.

PREPARATION TIME: 10–15 MINUTES

SIMMERING TIME: 10 MINUTES

SERVES: 8 (MAKES 2 CUPS)

1/2 cup	**Orange juice**
1/4 cup	**Maple syrup**
6 oz	**Cranberries**
1 medium	**Orange, peeled, segmented, and sliced**
1 Tbsp	**Fresh ginger root, diced**

Garnish:

1 Tbsp	**Mint leaves, fresh**

Heat juice and syrup in a sauce pan. When bubbling, add cranberries, orange, and ginger. Simmer 5–10 minutes until cranberries open. Remove from heat.

Serve warm or chilled. Garnish with mint leaves.

Per Serving   Calories: 52   % Fat Calories: 2.3%
Saturated fat: 0 grams   Fiber: 1.3 grams
Total Fat: 0.1 grams   Sodium: 0

Sautéed Fennel, Red Bell Pepper & Scallions

Enjoy the unique flavor the fennel adds to this dish.

PREPARATION TIME: 10 MINUTES

SERVES: SIDE DISH FOR 6

1 medium	**Fennel bulb**
1 medium	**Red bell pepper, sliced in long thin strips**
4 medium	**Scallions**
1 tsp	**Virgin olive oil**
1/4 tsp	**Sea salt**
1 tsp	**Dill weed**
1/4 cup	**Vegetable stock (See page 139)**

Trim away fennel root and stems from the bulb. Quarter fennel bulb lengthwise, then cut each quarter lengthwise into thirds. Cut pepper and chop scallions.

Just before serving dinner, heat sauté pan with oil over medium heat. Sauté fennel, pepper, salt and herbs for 2 minutes, stirring occasionally. Add stock and half the scallions. Heat 2 more minutes. Transfer to a serving platter and garnish with remaining scallions.

Per Serving   Calories: 34   % Fat Calories: 25%
Total Fat: 1 gram   Fiber: 0.8 grams
Saturated Fat: 0   Sodium: 120 mg

Sautéed Fennel, Red Bell Pepper & Scallions

23

Poached Pears in Hazelnut Cake

This is a beautiful winter dessert with a light, delicate flavor. After a 6-month cooking internship, I adapted this recipe from the dessert menu at Seattle's Four Seasons restaurant. Choose small ripe pears. Bartlett varieties work best. Lightly drizzle chocolate over the pear and cake, but save a piece of fine chocolate to savor, too.

PREPARATION TIME: 40 MINUTES
BAKING TIME: 20–25 MINUTES
SERVES: 6

Poaching pears:

6 cups	Apple cider or juice
6 medium	Prunes
1/2 tsp	Cloves, whole
1 medium	Cinnamon stick
1 medium	Orange
6 small	Bartlett pears
1/3 cup	Rum or brandy (optional)

Apricot sauce:

1 cup	Apricots, frozen or canned, rinsed
1 Tbsp	Candied ginger, minced
2 Tbsp	Maple syrup

Cake batter:

1/4 cup	Hazelnuts
3/4 cup	Whole wheat pastry flour
1/2 cup	All purpose flour
1/4 tsp	Sea salt
1/2 tsp	Baking soda
1 tsp	Baking powder
1/2 cup	Nonfat milk (or soy milk)
1/2 cup	Maple syrup
1/4 cup	Canola oil
1/2 tsp	Vanilla extract

Garnish:

2 oz	Fine chocolate
1/4 cup	Fresh berries

Pears

Preheat oven to 350°F.

Select 6 ovenproof bowls about 5 inches in diameter and 2 inches deep.

Poaching pears:
In a saucepan, combine cider, prunes, cloves and cinnamon. Squeeze juice from orange. Add juice and the remaining orange to saucepan. Bring to a gentle boil. Simmer 20 minutes. Strain out fruit and spices, reserving liquid.

Meanwhile, peel pears leaving the stems on. Cut the bottom flat. With a sharp knife, core out seeds from the base. Add pears and rum to spiced cider. Simmer 20 minutes until pears are tender but not too soft. Remove pears from cider and set aside to drain. (You can prepare the cider in advance, adding the pears and rum later.) Save the cider and serve as a beverage with dessert if desired.

Apricot sauce:
Drain or thaw apricots. Purée in a blender or food processor with candied ginger and maple syrup. Simmer in a saucepan for 20 minutes and set aside.

24

Cakes:

In a blender or food processor, grind hazelnuts into flour. With a fine mesh strainer, sift the dry ingredients then combine with the ground hazelnuts. In a separate bowl, combine the liquid cake ingredients and whisk until foamy. Gently add to the dry cake ingredients, stirring until batter is well mixed.

Spray individual bowls with canola oil and dust lightly with flour. Divide batter evenly into the 6 bowls. Gently sink a pear into the middle of the batter in each bowl. Bake for 20–25 minutes, until cake is golden. Allow cakes to cool on a wire rack for 10 minutes. Placing your hand over a cake, invert the bowl and gently remove the cake. Place cake right side up on a wire rack to cool completely. Repeat for remaining cakes. Cover in plastic wrap until ready to serve.

To serve, melt chocolate. Place cake with pear in the center of each dessert plate. Spoon 2 tablespoons of apricot sauce along the edge of each cake. Drizzle each cake with melted chocolate. Garnish with fresh berries.

Per Serving	Calories: 459	% Fat Calories: 30%
	Saturated Fat: 2.7 grams	Fiber: 7.6 grams
	Total Fat: 16.4 grams	Sodium: 263 mg

Poached Pears in Hazelnut Cake

Fruit Salad with Pears, Apples & Mandarin Oranges

Light Christmas Breakfast Menu

Nicole and I usually make this a light meal, keeping in mind the large Christmas Eve meal the night before and the Christmas dinner to follow. We buy or bake quality bread or bagels and serve them with our favorite marmalades (see Holiday Gifts section for recipes) and spreads. Fresh squeezed orange juice is served, along with coffee or tea. Then we rush off with the children to open presents.

Here's a menu for a light breakfast, followed by a full formal breakfast if that better suits your family tradition.

Fresh Squeezed Orange Juice

✤

Fruit Salad with Pears, Apples & Mandarin Oranges

✤

Whole Wheat Bagels & Raisin Cinnamon Bread

Leek & Roasted Red Pepper Spread

Kumquat Ginger Marmalade (see page 131)

✤

Coffee or Tea

Fruit Salad with Pears, Apples & Mandarin Oranges

Enjoy a quick and delicious salad on this busy but meaningful morning.

PREPARATION TIME: 10 MINUTES
SERVES: 6

1 medium	**Bartlett or Bosc pear, sliced**
1 medium	**Asian pear, peeled and sliced**
2 medium	**Apples, sliced**
14 ounces	**Mandarin orange slices, canned or fresh**
1 medium	**Lime, juiced**
1 cup	**Nonfat lemon yogurt (optional)**

Garnish:

1/2 cup	**Fresh mint**
1 small	**Pomegranate or fresh berries**

In a bowl, combine sliced pears, apples, and mandarin orange slices. Squeeze lime juice over them and toss together. Stir in yogurt if desired.

Garnish with fresh mint leaves and either pomegranate seeds or fresh berries.

Per Serving	Calories: 129	% Fat Calories: 4.7%
	Saturated Fat: 0.1 grams	Fiber: 5.7 grams
	Total Fat: 0.7 grams	Sodium: 36 mg

Leeks & Roasted Red Bell Pepper Spread

This is a tasty and nutritious spread that can be served with toasted bagels, or as a dip with colorful vegetable sticks.

PREPARATION TIME: 10 MINUTES
STRAINING TIME: 30 MINUTES
SERVES: 8

3 medium	Leeks
2 tsp	Extra virgin olive oil
1/4 tsp	Italian herbs, dried
1/8 tsp	Sea salt
2 medium	Red bell peppers, roasted
1 1/4 cups	Nonfat yogurt (optional)

Garnish:

Few sprigs	Fresh herbs

Cut the leek tops 1 inch above the color change from white to green, saving the greens for stock. Slice the leeks in half lengthwise, and rinse well to remove grit. Dice leeks. Heat a skillet over medium heat and add oil. Sauté leeks until soft. Add herbs, salt, and roasted peppers. Cover and simmer 5 minutes.

Purée in a blender with one cup of *yogurt cheese*. Serve chilled as a dip or spread. Garnish with fresh herbs.

Note:
To make one cup of nonfat *yogurt cheese*, pour 1 1/4 cups of nonfat yogurt into a fine strainer. Do not stir the yogurt. Let the whey (clear yellow liquid) slowly drip out of the strainer into a bowl and discard liquid. This usually takes 30 minutes, although you can leave the strainer in a bowl overnight in the refrigerator.

Per Serving	Calories: 68	% Fat Calories: 19%
	Saturated Fat: 0.2 grams	Fiber: 1.5 grams
	Total Fat: 1.5 grams	Sodium: 79 mg

Christmas Breakfast Menu

Coffee or Tea

✣

Fresh Squeezed Citrus Juice
with Sparkling Cider

✣

Scrambled Eggs or Tofu
with
Fennel, Mushrooms & Red Bell Pepper

✣

Red Potatoes with Rosemary & Garlic

✣

Christmas Pudding

Christmas Breakfast Preparation Plan

With the Christmas pudding prepared in advance, I allow 30–40 minutes to make this breakfast. For a shopping list, see page 141.

1–2 DAYS BEFORE CHRISTMAS BREAKFAST (30 MINUTES PREP TIME, PLUS 2 HOURS BAKING TIME)
- Soak prunes in water at least 6 hours or overnight.
- Make Christmas Pudding.

CHRISTMAS BREAKFAST (30–40 MINUTES PREP TIME)
- Preheat oven to 375°F.
- Cube and cook red potatoes. Toss with herbs.
- Place potatoes in an ovenproof dish and place in oven 15 minutes before serving.
- Prepare scrambled eggs or scrambled tofu.
- Heat store bought soy sausage (available in almost any major grocery store).
- To serve pudding, remove bowl or bowls by inverting onto a dessert plate. Warm brandy, pour over the pudding, and light for the flambé.

Scrambled Tofu

Scrambled Eggs or Tofu with Fennel, Mushrooms & Red Bell Pepper

Combine this healthy, colorful entrée with roasted red potatoes and soy sausage for a wonderful holiday breakfast. During June of 1997, I had great fun working at Café Flora, one of Seattle's great vegetarian restaurants. One of the busiest aspects of that job was cooking brunch, in particular the popular Wild Mushroom Omelettes and Scrambled Tofu with Wild Mushrooms. Even today, I think back to the great group of people I worked with whenever I prepare this dish.

PREPARATION TIME: 20 MINUTES
SERVES: 6

1 Tbsp	Virgin olive oil
1 medium	Onion, diced
2 cups	Mushrooms, shiitake, sliced
1/2 tsp	Sea salt
1/8 tsp	Black pepper, ground
1/2 tsp	Italian herbs, dried
3 cups	Fennel bulb and stalks, diced
1 large	Red bell pepper, diced
1/2–1 tsp	Turmeric, ground
2 Tbsp	Vegetable stock, or water
2 cups	Egg whites, beaten, or egg substitute–such as Egg Beaters®
	Or,
1 lb	Tofu, firm

Garnish:

3 Tbsp	Fennel leaves, chopped

Heat a sauté pan over medium-high heat and add oil. Sauté onion and mushrooms with salt and pepper for 2–3 minutes. Add dried herbs and fennel. Cook over medium heat for 2 minutes. Add red bell pepper, turmeric, to taste, and stock. Cook for 2 more minutes.

Pour the beaten egg whites or egg beaters into sauté. Stir with a spatula, flipping small egg sections at a time, without mashing eggs. When cooked but still moist, transfer with the spatula to a serving plate. Garnish with fennel leaves.

Vegan Option:
Substitute tofu for eggs. With paper towels, pat the tofu dry, then crumble it with your hands. Sauté over medium-high heat as you would the egg whites.

Per Serving	Calories: 145	% Fat Calories: 15%
	Saturated Fat: 0.4 grams	Fiber: 3.3 grams
	Total Fat: 2.7 grams	Sodium: 410 mg

Red Potatoes with Rosemary & Garlic

You can prepare the potatoes in advance. For an added treat, serve with soy sausage (many delicious brands are available in major grocery stores).

PREPARATION TIME: 10 MINUTES
SIMMERING TIME: 20 MINUTES
BAKING TIME: 15 MINUTES
SERVES: 6

18 small	**Red potatoes**
2 Tbsp	**Virgin olive oil**
1/2 tsp	**Sea salt**
1/4 tsp	**Black pepper, freshly ground**
1 Tbsp	**Rosemary, chopped**
4 medium	**Garlic cloves, minced**

Garnish:

3 Tbsp	**Fennel leaves, chopped**

Preheat oven to 375°F.

Quarter potatoes. Put in a stock pot, cover with water, and bring to a boil. Reduce heat and simmer until potatoes are nearly cooked, but not soft and crumbly, about 20 minutes. Drain potatoes.

In a large bowl, add nearly cooked potatoes and toss with oil, salt, pepper, rosemary, and garlic. Transfer to an ovenproof pan and bake 15 minutes. Garnish with fennel leaves.

Per Serving		
	Calories: 315	% Fat Calories: 14%
	Total Fat: 5.0 grams	Fiber: 5.6 grams
	Saturated Fat: 0.7 grams	Sodium: 186 mg

Christmas Pudding

Try this healthier version of a traditional holiday dessert. While it remains moderately high-fat, it is made with healthy fat sources (nuts), and is packed with nutrients and antioxidants.

PREPARATION TIME: 30 MINUTES
BAKING TIME: 2 HOURS
SERVES: 8

6 oz	**Prunes, pitted**
1/2 cup	**Water**
1 cup	**Dried cherries**
1 cup	**Raisins**
1/2 cup	**Pecans, ground finely**
1/2 cup	**Almonds, finely ground**
1 medium	**Orange, juiced**
2 Tbsp	**Grated orange rind**
1/3 cup	**Brandy, or rum (or water)**
1 Tbsp	**Canola oil**
1/4 tsp	**Allspice**
1/4 tsp	**Ginger powder**
1/4 tsp	**Ground cinnamon**
1/4 tsp	**Nutmeg**
Flambé:	
1/4 cup	**Brandy or rum (optional)**
Or	**Glaze: (See glaze recipe on page 75)**

Soak prunes in water overnight, preferably 12 hours.

Preheat oven to 300°F.

Purée prunes and their soaking liquid in a food processor. Add half the dried cherries and raisins. Purée again.

Mix in ground nuts, orange juice, orange rind, brandy, oil, spices, and remaining dried fruit. Mix well.

Spray a 1-quart ovenproof bowl or, 8 1/2-cup pudding bowls generously with canola oil. Spoon pudding mixture equally into bowl(s)–allowing 1/2–1 inch of headroom on top. Cover with foil.

Place pudding bowl(s) in an oven pan. Pour enough water in pan to come 2 inches up the outer sides of the pudding bowl(s). Steam in the oven for 2 hours.

To serve, free bowl edges, and turn onto a serving dish or individual plates.

Flambé or Glaze:
For flambé, heat brandy in a pan on medium heat until just bubbling (don't overcook, or brandy won't light). Light brandy and pour over pudding(s).
For glaze, make glaze as indicated on page 75. Drizzle over cake(s).

Per Serving		
(with flambé)	Calories: 436	% Fat Calories: 38%
	Saturated Fat: 1.6 grams	Fiber: 6 grams
	Total Fat: 19.1 grams	Sodium: 43 mg

Christmas Pudding

Christmas Dinner Menu

This is our main Christmas day meal. In the evening, we relax and enjoy the endless leftovers in the refrigerator. You certainly can serve this at supper time for your special meal, too. Most of the preparation for this meal is done in advance, allowing you to enjoy your holiday and your guests.

Two-Colored Beet & Leek Soup

✣

Christmas Crêpes

✣

Whipped Yams with Ginger

Green Beans with Mushrooms & Kale

Cranberry Sauce with Ginger & Orange

✣

Bûche de Noël

Christmas Dinner Preparation Plan

Allow 5 hours of total preparation time. I enjoy preparing the soup, crêpes, and sauces a few days in advance. The Bûche de Noël freezes well for several days, too. For a shopping list, see page 142.

1–3 DAYS BEFORE CHRISTMAS DINNER (3 HOURS PREP TIME)
- Make two-colored soup.
- Make crêpes (these freeze well).
- Make crêpe filling.
- Prepare cranberry sauce.
- Make Bûche de Noël. (Chocolate Sponge Cake.)

After you prepare these items, seal them separately and store in the refrigerator.

DAY OF CHRISTMAS DINNER (30 MINUTES PREP TIME)
- Bake yams (when soft, turn off the oven, remove skin, and leave in the oven to keep warm).
- Remove stems from green beans, slice mushrooms and kale, and measure almond slices. Set aside to sauté later.
- Fill and roll crêpes and place in baking dish.

1 HOUR BEFORE SERVING CHRISTMAS DINNER
- Open wine to breathe, or have sparkling cider chilling in the refrigerator.
- Remove cake from the refrigerator.
- Preheat oven to 375°F.

25 MINUTES BEFORE SERVING CHRISTMAS DINNER
- Pour chilled soups into pitchers, and serve in individual bowls.
- Place crêpes in the oven. Bake 20 minutes.
- Enjoy soup over 10–15 minutes.

10–15 MINUTES BEFORE SERVING CHRISTMAS DINNER
- Prepare green beans with mushrooms and kale.
- Whip yams and season.
- Place cranberry sauce on the table.

WHEN SERVING
- Pipe whipped yams onto individual plates with a piping bag, or spoon into a serving bowl.
- Garnish crêpes with sprigs of fresh parsley.
- Serve green beans on individual plates, or place in a serving dish and garnish.

Steven preparing crêpes (photo by Kim Zumwalt)

Christmas Dinner

Two-Colored Beet & Leek Soup

Serve these soups hot or cold. They are delicious and add festive color to a holiday meal.

PREPARATION TIME: 30–40 MINUTES
SIMMERING TIME: 30 MINUTES
SERVES: 6–8

Beet soup:

1 Tbsp	Virgin olive oil
1 medium	Onion, chopped
1/2 tsp	Italian herbs, dried
1/4 tsp	Salt
1 medium	Carrot, diced
1 medium	Russet potato, cut into 1/2-inch cubes
4 cups	Vegetable stock (see page 139)
3 medium	Garlic cloves, minced
4 medium	Beets, peeled and cut into 1/2-inch cubes
1 Tbsp	Lemon juice, fresh

Leek soup:

2 medium	Leeks
2 medium	Russet potatoes
1 Tbsp	Virgin olive oil
1 medium	Onion, peeled and chopped
1/2 tsp	Sea salt
2 cups	Nonfat milk (or soy milk)
2 cups	Vegetable stock (see page 139)

Garnish:

1 Tbsp	Lemon rind, grated

Beet soup:
Heat pan over medium-high heat and add oil. Sauté onion until yellow, about 3 minutes. Add herbs, salt, carrot, and potato. Heat 3 minutes. Add stock, garlic, and beets. Bring to a low boil, then reduce heat and simmer, 20–30 minutes until beets and potato are soft. Remove from heat and purée in a blender with lemon juice.

Leek soup:
Clean and dice whites of leeks and first 1-inch into green. Peel and dice potato. Heat pan over medium-high heat and add oil. Sauté leeks, potatoes, onion, and salt about 5 minutes or until leeks and onion are yellow and soft, but not browned. Add milk and stock. Reduce heat and simmer 20 minutes. Remove from heat and purée in a blender.

Two colored soup:
Pour each soup into a separate pitcher. Simultaneously pour soups into opposite edges of each soup bowl. Garnish each bowl with grated lemon. Serve warm or chilled.

Per Serving: Calories: 174   % Fat Calories: 25%
Saturated Fat: 0.8 grams   Fiber: 4.0 grams
Total Fat: 5.0 grams   Sodium: 992 mg

Christmas Crêpes

These colorful crêpes can be prepared in advance and put in the oven twenty minutes prior to serving. Crêpes store nicely in the freezer. Cooking crêpes for the first time can be tricky–extra batter makes the process easier.

PREPARATION TIME: 90 MINUTES
BAKING TIME: 20 MINUTES
SERVES: 6 (MAKES 12 6-INCH CRÊPES)

Crêpes:

1 cup	Whole wheat pastry flour
1/4 tsp	Sea salt
1 tsp	Italian herbs, dried
1 1/3 cups	Nonfat milk (or 1 cup of soy milk + 1/3 cup water)
3 Tbsp	Parsley, finely chopped
3 large	Egg whites (or 2 Tbsp ground flax seeds + 3/4 cup water)
1 Tbsp	Canola oil

Filling:

2 medium	Russet potatoes, peeled and cubed
1/4 tsp	Sea salt
1 Tbsp	Extra virgin olive oil
1/4 cup	Nonfat milk, or soy milk
1 Tbsp	Virgin olive oil
1 medium	Onion, diced
2 medium	Carrots, diced
1/4 tsp	Sea salt
1 tsp	Italian herbs, dried
1/4 cup	White wine
1 medium	Red bell pepper, diced
6 medium	Scallions, sliced thinly
1/2 cup	Nonfat mozzarella cheese (or soy)
1/2 cup	Parmesan cheese (or soy)
1/2 cup	Vegetable stock (see page 139)

Garnish:

1/4 cup	Parsley, finely chopped
3 Tbsp	Sliced almonds

Preheat oven to 375°F.

Crêpes:
In a bowl, mix flour, salt, and dried herbs. In a separate bowl, whisk together milk, parsley, egg whites, and canola oil. Mix liquid with dry ingredients.

Heat a crêpe pan or a small non-stick skillet over medium-high heat. Coat the pan for 1 second with canola oil spray just before adding the batter. Pour 1/8 cup of batter into hot pan and tip pan to spread it. Cook crêpes until golden, about 20–30 seconds for each side. Repeat the process until 12 crêpes are made.

Filling:
Boil prepared potatoes until soft. Drain, then whip or mash with salt, extra virgin olive oil, and milk. Set aside.

Heat a pan over medium-high heat and add virgin olive oil. Sauté onions, carrots, salt and herbs for 2–3 minutes, until onions are yellow and soft. Add wine, stir, and heat 1–2 minutes. Add pepper and scallions and cook 2 minutes. Remove from heat. Stir in 1/4 cup mozzarella and 1/4 cup parmesan cheese. Stir in vegetable stock. Fold in mashed potatoes. Fill and roll crêpes with above mixture. Place in an ovenproof pan. Sprinkle remaining cheese and almonds over crêpes. Bake 20 minutes. Garnish with sliced pepper and parsley, and serve.

Vegan Option:
Substitute soy cheese for dairy cheese in the filling.
In place of egg whites, grind 2 tablespoons of flax seeds and mix with 3/4 cup of water. Mix with the rest of the crêpe ingredients to make the batter. Follow remaining directions.

Per Serving	Calories: 294	% Fat Calories: 36%
	Saturated Fat: 2.3 grams	Fiber: 6.0 grams
	Total Fat: 11.9 grams	Sodium: 632 mg

Christmas Crêpes (photo by Kim Zumwalt)

41

Whipped Yams with Ginger

Piped on a plate, whipped yams are colorful and elegant. It's a nice substitute for the traditional mashed potato dish and adds a bundle of healthy nutrients and antioxidants to your meal.

PREPARATION TIME: 10–15 MINUTES
BAKING TIME: 60–80 MINUTES
SERVES: 6

4 medium	Yams
1 tsp	Ginger powder
1/2 tsp	Sea salt
1 cup	Nonfat milk, or soy milk

Preheat oven to 375°F. Poke yam with a fork and bake until very soft, 40–60 minutes. Remove skin and whip yams until smooth. Stir in ginger, salt, and milk. Place yam in a covered baking dish and keep warm in the oven.

To serve, place in a serving dish, or pipe potatoes (see page 10) in a circular fashion directly on guests' plates.

Per Serving	Calories: 106	% Fat Calories: 3%
	Saturated Fat: 0.1 grams	Fiber: 2.6 grams
	Total Fat: 0.3 grams	Sodium: 210 mg

Cranberry Sauce with Ginger & Orange

(See page 22)

Green Beans with Mushrooms & Kale

PREPARATION TIME: 10 MINUTES
SERVES: 6

4 cups	Green beans
1 cup	Shiitake mushrooms, sliced
1 cup	Purple kale, finely sliced
1 Tbsp	Virgin olive oil
1/8 tsp	Sea salt
1/2 tsp	Dill weed
1/4 cup	Vegetable stock (see page 139)
Garnish:	
2 Tbsp	Sliced almonds

Remove stem from green beans. Remove shiitake stems. Discard stems. Slice mushrooms. Slice kale into thin slivers.

6 minutes before serving, heat a sauté pan over medium-high heat and add oil. Sauté mushrooms with salt for 2 minutes. Add green beans and kale and stir, reduce heat to medium, add dill weed and stock. Heat 2–3 minutes. Serve directly on plates or on a serving dish. Garnish with sliced almonds.

Per Serving	Calories: 101	% Fat Calories: 32%
	Saturated Fat: 0.5 grams	Fiber: 4.3 grams
	Total Fat: 4.1 grams	Sodium: 100 mg

Bûche de Noël

Bûche de Noël

This is a glorious, vegan sponge cake, assembled like the traditional yule-log. It has a chestnut filling and is covered with rich, dark chocolate. Nicole makes this special treat every Christmas. Decorated with holly leaves it is elegant as well as delicious. (Please note that we use plastic holly as holly leaves are poisonous.) You can buy cooked and peeled chestnuts, or spend an extra hour cooking and peeling them yourself. Already assembled, this cake freezes very well.

PREPARATION TIME: 1 HOUR WITH COOKED AND PEELED CHESTNUTS
BAKING TIME: 15 MINUTES
SERVES: 10–12

Filling:

10 oz	Chestnuts, cooked and peeled
1 Tbsp	Nonfat milk (or soy milk)
3 Tbsp	Sugar
3 Tbsp	Dark rum (or milk)
1/2 tsp	Vanilla extract

Cake:

1/2 cup	Sugar
1/2 cup	Whole wheat pastry flour
1/2 cup	All purpose flour
1/2 tsp	Sea salt
1 tsp	Baking powder
1 1/2 tsp	Baking soda
1/4 cup	Cocoa powder
3/4 cup	Nonfat milk or soy milk
3 1/2 Tbsp	Canola oil
1/2 cup	White wine (or milk)
2 tsp	Vanilla extract

Icing:

4 oz	Semi-sweet chocolate
2 Tbsp	Hot water
3 Tbsp	Sugar

Topping:

1 cup	Nonfat or non-dairy whipped topping, pressurized

Preheat oven to 350°F.

Purée the filling ingredients and set aside.

Cover a large cookie sheet with parchment or wax paper, then spray it with canola oil. Combine dry cake ingredients and sift through a fine mesh strainer. In a separate bowl, whisk together liquid cake ingredients. Gently pour liquid ingredients into dry and stir until well mixed.

Pour the batter onto the prepared cookie sheet and spread it evenly so that you have a 14x9-inch rectangle. Bake for 10–15 minutes. Allow the cake to cool for 5 minutes, then roll it up lengthwise (like a jelly-roll) with the parchment paper still attached to it. Wait 1 minute then unroll the cake and spread the filling evenly over the cake surface (don't worry if the cake cracks, it won't show in the end). Roll the cake up again, while removing the parchment. Allow the roll to cool.

With a bread knife, slice a 3-inch piece off each end at a 45 degree angle. Gently transfer the large piece onto a serving platter. Place the small pieces to either side of the roll with the slanted end showing outward. The cake should now look like a log with 2 cut-off branches.

In a double boiler, melt chocolate. In a separate sauce pan, heat water and sugar until all the granules are dissolved. Remove chocolate from heat. Stir in the hot liquid until well mixed. Spread over the cake surface, leaving the branch and log ends visible. As the icing cools, draw vertical lines along the log and limbs, making the icing look like bark. Decorate with holly leaves. Serve each portion with whipped topping.

Per Serving	Calories: 236	% Fat Calories: 31%
	Saturated Fat: 2 grams	Fiber: 2 grams
	Total Fat: 8 grams	Sodium: 261 mg

New Year's Eve Dinner

New Year's Eve is a night we spend with friends and family chatting, dancing, and bringing in the New Year. A filling but not heavy dinner will provide lasting energy and a good start to your evening. In the Orient, they celebrate the New Year with passion. Invite friends over for Oriental food. It is a great way to start your celebrations.

New Year's Eve Dinner Menu

Sushi Rice Rolls

✤

Won Ton Soup

✤

Sichuan Seitan Stir-Fry

✤

Snow Peas & Wild Mushrooms with Ginger

✤

Chocolate Soufflé with Raspberry Sauce
or
Chocolate Mousse

✤

Sparkling Cider or Champagne

New Year's Eve Dinner Preparation Plan

To prepare for this New Year's dinner party, I allow one hour the day before and two hours the day of the party. I leave the final assembly for the party. For a shopping list, see page 143.

1 DAY BEFORE NEW YEAR'S EVE (1 HOUR PREP TIME)
- Bake yams until very soft for the soufflé.
- Make stock for won ton soup.
- Make seitan marinade.
- Prepare raspberry sauce, or chocolate mousse.

After you prepare these items, seal separately and store in the refrigerator.

DAY OF DINNER PARTY (2 HOURS PREP TIME)
- Cook rice for sushi rolls. Steam asparagus and bell peppers. Set aside to cool.
- Scoop cooked yam filling from skin. Blend with vanilla, Grand Marnier, oil, salt, and milk. Stir in cocoa powder. Return to the refrigerator.
- Separate egg whites for soufflé. Cover, and store in the refrigerator.
- Place champagne or sparkling cider in the refrigerator.
- Remove stems from snow peas, slice mushrooms, and assemble ingredients for snow pea and mushroom stir-fry.
- Slice and steam eggplant. Slice leeks, ginger, broccoli, and peppers for Sichuan seitan. Assemble remaining ingredients.
- Slice kale for soup and sauté won tons. Set aside.
- Assemble sushi rolls, cover and set aside. If you've never rolled these before, give yourself a little extra time, and make a double batch. It's fun once you get the hang of it.
- Prepare and assemble won tons. Cover and set aside.

30 MINUTES BEFORE PARTY
- Transfer sushi rolls to a serving dish and have ready to serve when guests arrive.

20 MINUTES BEFORE SERVING DINNER
- Heat won ton soup stock, add kale and won tons 5 minutes before serving soup.
- Bring water to a boil for soba noodles, then turn heat off and cover.

TO SERVE DINNER
- Serve and enjoy soup. Then, return to kitchen for final 10-minute assembly.
- Reheat water to a boil and start soba noodles.
- Start Sichuan seitan stir-fry.
- Sauté snow pea and mushroom dish.
- Preheat oven to 375°F for dessert.
- Garnish serving plates and serve.

TO SERVE DESSERT
- Beat egg whites, assemble chocolate soufflé, and bake.
- Garnish dessert plates and serve soufflé immediately as it comes out of the oven.

Sushi Rice Rolls

Sushi Rice Rolls

These are fun hors d'oeuvres to make and eat. Vary the filling with what looks best in the market. Offer chopsticks, or enjoy eating with your fingers.

<small>PREPARATION TIME: 30 MINUTES
RICE STEAMING TIME: 40–45 MINUTES
SERVES: 6–8</small>

1 cup	Brown rice, short grain
2 cups	Water
3 Tbsp	Rice vinegar
2 tsp	Soy sauce, low-sodium
1 tsp	Sugar
3/4 cup	Avocado, mashed (about 2 small or 1 large)
1 Tbsp	Lemon juice
16 medium	Asparagus spears
1 medium	Red bell pepper, sliced into long thin strips
6 sheets	Nori seaweed sheets, toasted

Garnish:

1 small	Cucumber, sliced
1/4 cup	Rice vinegar
1/2 tsp	Soy sauce, low-sodium
1 tsp	Sesame seeds

Bring rice and water to a boil, then simmer until done, about 40–45 minutes. In a small bowl, combine vinegar, soy sauce, and sugar. Stir into cooked rice. Set aside to cool.

Mash avocado. Add lemon juice. Set aside. Steam asparagus and bell pepper strips until al dente, then dip in ice water to arrest the cooking process. Drain and set aside.

Place a nori sheet on a double layer of papertowels or a Japanese mat. Spread 1/3 cup of rice over the half of the nori sheet closest to you. Spread out 2 tablespoons of avocado over the rice in a 1-inch wide horizontal strip. Place 2 strips of pepper and 1–2 asparagus spears over the avocado (see photo below).

Starting from the bottom, roll nori sheet into a tube, pulling tightly to compact filling. With a sharp knife, cut the tube crosswise into 1-inch slices. Lay each slice upright on a serving platter. Repeat the process with the 5 remaining nori sheets.

Soak cucumber slices and remaining asparagus for a few minutes in a bowl with rice vinegar and soy sauce. Drain cucumber and asparagus and serve with sushi. Garnish with sesame seeds.

Per Serving

Calories: 177	% Fat Calories: 25%
Saturated Fat: 0.9 grams	Fiber: 2.7 grams
Total Fat: 5.3 grams	Sodium: 700 mg

Preparing Sushi Rice Rolls

Won Ton Soup

This soup has a rich, yet delicate flavor. Vary the vegetable ingredients inside the won tons as you like. You can easily make extra won tons, saving them for another day.

PREPARATION TIME: 30–40 MINUTES
SERVES: 6–8

1 Tbsp	**Ginger root, minced**
1/2 small	**Onion, minced**
2 tsp	**Canola oil**
1 cup	**Broccoli flowerets, finely chopped**
6 medium	**Garlic cloves, minced**
1/4 lb	**Tofu, firm, finely diced**
18 4-inch	**Won ton wrappers**
2 cups	**Shiitake mushrooms, sliced**
1/2 tsp	**Canola oil**
1 tsp	**Rice vinegar**
6 cups	**Water**
2 Tbsp	**Miso**
2 cups	**Kale, sliced in long, thin strips**
1 tsp	**Lemon juice**

Garnish:

Few	**Sprigs of parsley**

Sauté ginger root and onion in oil over medium-high heat for 2–3 minutes. Add broccoli, garlic, and tofu and cook another 3 minutes. Set aside to cool.

Spread won ton wrappers on a dry surface. Place 1 1/2 teaspoons of sauté mixture into the center of each won ton. Brush water along outer edge of won tons. Fold in half, forming a triangle. Press edges firmly together using fingers or a fork. Spray for 1–2 seconds with canola oil. Heat a large skillet. Spray with canola oil and sauté won tons until lightly golden on each side. Set won tons aside separately so they don't stick together.

Heat a large soup pot over medium-high heat and add oil. Sauté mushrooms for 2 minutes. Add vinegar and 6 cups of hot water. Bring to a slow boil. Reduce heat and simmer for 5 minutes. Dissolve miso in a few tablespoons of the stock. Add to soup. Stir in kale and won tons. Simmer 3–4 minutes, add lemon juice, and serve.

Garnish each bowl with sprigs of parsley.

Per Serving	Calories: 321	% Fat Calories: 12%
	Saturated Fat: 0.6 grams	Fiber: 8 grams
	Total Fat: 4.5 grams	Sodium: 750 mg

Sichuan Seitan Stir-fry

Sichuan (also spelled szechwan) cooking originates in a region in China that relies on garlic, red pepper, leeks, ginger, and vinegar to flavor its cuisine. You can serve this with brown rice or soba noodles. Look for seitan in Oriental food stores. You can substitute tofu or garbanzo beans for seitan, using the same marinating sauce.

PREPARATION TIME: 20 MINUTES
SIMMER TIME: 5–6 MINUTES
SERVES: 6

Marinade:

1/2 Tbsp	Miso paste
1/2 cup	Hot water
1 tsp	Corn starch
2 Tbsp	Rice vinegar
1/2–1 tsp	Chili-Garlic paste
1 Tbsp	Diced ginger root
1 Tbsp	Soy sauce, low-sodium
15 oz	Seitan (braised wheat gluten)

Stir-Fry:

3/4 cup	Cashews, chopped
3 medium	Japanese eggplants (or one regular eggplant)
2 medium	Leeks
2 cups	Broccoli flowerets, sliced in thin strips
2 medium	Red bell peppers, sliced in thin strips
2 tsp	Canola oil
1/4 cup	Fresh cilantro, chopped
15 oz	Japanese soba noodles

Garnish:

Few	Sprigs of cilantro

Dissolve miso paste in hot water. Dissolve corn starch in vinegar. Combine dissolved miso, corn starch, chili paste, ginger root, soy sauce, and seitan. (Chili paste hotness varies greatly; add to taste.) Marinate seitan for several hours in the refrigerator–best if marinated for 1–2 days.

Preheat oven to 300°F. Roast cashews for 5–6 minutes or, microwave for 1 minute.

Bring a large pot of water to boil for noodles.

Slice eggplant lengthwise into finger sized pieces. Steam them 5 minutes to pre-cook. Remove leek tops and tiny roots, saving the white and first inch of light green. Cut leeks in half lengthwise, rinse, and slice finely. Slice broccoli and bell pepper.

Put noodles in boiling water for 5–10 minutes, following package directions. Meanwhile, heat a sauté pan, add oil, and sauté leeks, broccoli, and peppers for 2 minutes over medium-high heat. Add eggplant, cilantro, and seitan marinade. Simmer 3–4 minutes. Don't overcook vegetables.

Place noodles on a large serving dish. Mix with half the stir fry, then pour remaining stir-fry on top. Garnish with roasted cashews and cilantro sprigs.

Per Serving	Calories: 634	% Fat Calories: 18.6%
	Saturated Fat: 2.5 grams	Fiber: 6.2 grams
	Total Fat: 14 grams	Sodium: 611 mg

Snow Peas & Wild Mushrooms with Ginger

This is an easy-to-make side dish. Add tofu or beans, serve with rice, and you have a full meal.

PREPARATION TIME: 10 MINUTES
SERVES: 6

1/2 tsp	Canola oil (or sesame oil)
3 cups	Mixed mushrooms (shiitake, chanterelles, oyster, etc.), sliced
2 Tbsp	Ginger root, peeled and sliced into 1/2-inch thin match sticks
1/2 tsp	Ginger powder
1/2 tsp	Cardamom, ground
1 tsp	Corn starch
2 tsp	Rice vinegar
1/2 tsp	Soy sauce, low-sodium
3 cups	Snow peas, fresh or frozen
15 oz	Baby corn, canned

Heat a sauté pan over medium-high heat and add oil. Sauté mushrooms, ginger root, ginger powder, and cardamom for 2 minutes, stirring occasionally.

Dissolve corn starch in vinegar and soy sauce. Add corn starch mixture, snow peas and baby corn to sauté. Heat 2–3 minutes. Remove from heat and serve. (Don't overcook the vegetables.)

Per Serving	Calories: 178	% Fat Calories: 10%
	Saturated Fat: 0.4 grams	Fiber: 7.2 grams
	Total Fat: 2.1 grams	Sodium: 206 mg

Snow Peas & Wild Mushrooms with Ginger

Chocolate Soufflé

Here is an enticing dessert, great to accent an evening of dancing, fun, or romance. You can't taste the yams, but they add texture, moisture, and richness to the soufflé. Bake and serve immediately, or, bake in advance, refrigerate, and serve chilled.

PREPARATION TIME: 20 MINUTES
BAKING TIME: 30 MINUTES
SERVES: 6

1 1/2 cups	Yams
1/2 tsp	Vanilla extract
3 Tbsp	Grand Marnier
1/4 cup	Almond oil (or canola oil)
1/8 tsp	Sea salt
1/3 cup	Sugar
1/2 cup	Nonfat milk (or soy milk)
1/3 cup	Cocoa powder, Dutch processed, sifted
2 Tbsp	Flour, all purpose, sifted
6 large	Egg whites
1/3 cup	Sugar
2 Tbsp	Water

Garnish:

2 Tbsp	Orange zest, grated
1 cup	Raspberry sauce (see page 55)
1/2 cup	Fresh berries

Preheat oven to 375°F.

Bake or microwave 1 large yam until very soft (about 40–50 minutes in the oven or 10–12 minutes in the microwave). Set aside to cool. Measure 1 1/2 cups of peeled yam and mix in a blender with vanilla, Grand Marnier, oil, salt, sugar, and milk. Stir in sifted cocoa powder and flour.

Beat egg whites until they form soft peaks. Meanwhile, combine 1/3 cup of sugar and water in a sauce pan. Cook over medium-high heat for 2–3 minutes. Remove from heat before it caramelizes and turns brown. Carefully pour heated sugar to egg whites while beating at high speed for 1 minute. (*Use caution as the syrup can splatter and burn.*)

Gently fold the chocolate batter into egg whites. Don't over mix or the soufflé won't rise.

Grease a round soufflé dish (9-inch in diameter, 4-inch high) with canola oil spray. Pour soufflé into dish. Bake for 30 minutes, until the top browns and a toothpick comes out clean. Garnish serving plates with fresh berries. Drizzle 1/2 cup of raspberry sauce over the dessert plates. Cut soufflé and serve immediately. Save remaining sauce to drizzle over soufflé at the table. Garnish each portion with orange zest.

Per Serving	Calories: 370	% Fat Calories: 25%
	Saturated Fat: 1 gram	Fiber: 6.7 grams
	Total Fat: 10 grams	Sodium: 117 mg

Raspberry Sauce

Raspberry sauce can be used with many recipes. It adds a lovely touch and flavor to this chocolate soufflé.

PREPARATION TIME: 10 MINUTES
SIMMERING TIME: 10 MINUTES
MAKES: 1 CUP OF SAUCE

2 1/2 cups	Raspberries, frozen or fresh
1/3 cup	Sugar
1/8 tsp	Sea salt
2 tsp	Port wine
2 Tbsp	Lemon juice

Garnish:

Few	Sprigs fresh mint
1/2 cup	Fresh berries (raspberries, sliced strawberries, etc.)

Heat raspberries and sugar over medium heat in a sauce pan until bubbling. Simmer 5 minutes. Pour through a large sieve to remove the seeds. Combine wine, lemon juice, and salt. Stir until dissolved. Add to raspberry sauce. Simmer until thickened, about 5–10 minutes. Set aside to cool.

When serving sauce, garnish with mint leaves and fresh berries.

Per serving	Calories: 73	% Fat Calories: 3%
	Saturated Fat: 0	Fiber: 0
	Total fat: 0.3 grams	Sodium: 18 mg

Chocolate Soufflé with Raspberry Sauce

Chocolate Mousse

Chocolate Mousse

Here is Nicole's vegan chocolate mouse recipe. Fortune cookies add extra fun to eating this rich dessert.

PREPARATION TIME: 15 MINUTES
SERVES: 6

12 oz	Tofu, silken
4 oz	Semisweet chocolate chips
2/3 cup	Maple syrup
1 tsp	Powdered coffee, instant
1/8 tsp	Sea salt
1/2 cup	Cocoa powder
3 Tbsp	Grand Marnier
1 Tbsp	Orange peel, grated

Garnish:

1 Tbsp	Orange peel, grated
6 slices	Orange, thinly sliced
6 regular	Fortune cookies

Rinse and drain the tofu in a sieve. Set aside.

In a food processor or blender, process chocolate until finely chopped.

In a saucepan, heat maple syrup and stir in coffee and salt. With the food processor running, slowly pour in the hot syrup and process for another 1–2 minutes until you notice the chocolate has melted.

Add remaining ingredients and process until smooth. Pour into a medium sized serving bowl or into individual dessert bowls and garnish with grated orange peel. Chill until ready to serve. Serve with fortune cookies.

Per Serving	Calories: 202	% Fat Calories: 29.4%
	Saturated Fat: 3.2 grams	Fiber: 3.2 grams
	Total Fat: 7.0 grams	Sodium: 41 mg

Passover Meal

Passover celebrates many aspects in life. It welcomes re-birth as winter passes over into spring. It celebrates the Jewish departure from Egyptian slavery and darkness into freedom in the land of Israel. When the Israelites escaped Egypt, they left in a hurry. There was no time to bake real bread, hence matzo meal is commonly served in many forms over Passover. Passover is a great time for spring-cleaning. Sweep and clean every corner and every cupboard. Throw away old grains and spices. Prepare to start a new, richer life.

Passover Meal Menu

Borscht

❖

Passover Kishke

❖

Turkish Salad

❖

Broccoli with Lemon Sauce

❖

Fruit Compôte
with
Mint Tea

Passover Meal Preparation Plan

This meal follows traditional Jewish religious food laws for the Passover Seder. Allow 4 hours of total preparation time. For a shopping list, see page 144.

PREP TIME 1–2 DAYS IN ADVANCE (2 HOURS PREP TIME)
- Prepare kishke rolls. (Don't bake until ready to serve.)
- Make borscht.
- Make gravy.

Wrap the rolls in foil and seal borscht and gravy in separate containers. Store in the refrigerator.

DAY OF MEAL (2 HOURS PREP TIME)
- Prepare the fruit compôte, and simmer 1 hour.
- Slice broccoli into long, thin spears and make the lemon sauce.
- Prepare Turkish salad. Store in the refrigerator.
- 1 hour prior to serving your Passover meal, preheat the oven to 350°F and place the kishke rolls in the oven.

20 MINUTES BEFORE THE MEAL
- Reheat the borscht.
- Garnish fruit compôte and place in a serving bowl in the refrigerator.
- Reheat the gravy on low heat, adding stock if it is too thick.
- Serve borscht.

10 MINUTES BEFORE SERVING THE MEAL
- Reheat the lemon sauce on low heat.
- Steam spinach leaves until lightly cooked.
- Boil water and steam broccoli until al dente.
- Remove kishke from the oven, unroll foil, transfer to a serving plate, and wrap rolls with steamed spinach leaves.

TO SERVE
- Transfer gravy to a serving bowl.
- Add Mandarin slices to the Turkish salad if not done previously.
- Place steamed broccoli in a serving bowl, and drizzle on lemon sauce.

Borscht

Here's a low-fat version of the classic Russian winter soup. If not served over the Jewish Passover, it can be served as a meal with a hearty rye bread. If you don't find beets with greens, you can substitute a cup of Swiss chard or an extra cup of cabbage. This soup is wonderful hot or chilled.

PREPARATION TIME: 20 MINUTES
SIMMERING TIME: 20 MINUTES
SERVES: 8

4 medium	Beets, with chopped greens
1 Tbsp	Canola oil
1 large	Onion, diced
1 tsp	Sea salt
3 medium	Carrots, cubed
2 medium	Potatoes, cubed
6 medium	Garlic cloves, chopped
1/4 tsp	Caraway seeds, crushed
8 oz	Tomatoes, canned or fresh, chopped
6 cups	Warm water
1 cup	Cabbage, chopped

Garnish with:

3/4 cup	Nonfat yogurt (optional)
1/4 cup	Chives, sliced

Rinse the beets and cut greens off the roots. Set beet greens aside. Drop the beet roots into boiling water for 1 minute (to help remove skins). Allow to cool, then peel.

Heat a large saucepan over medium heat and add oil. Sauté onion with salt for 2–3 minutes, until onions appear slightly golden.

Cut the carrots, potatoes, and two of the beets into small cubes. Grate the other two beets. Add carrots, potatoes, cubed and grated beets, garlic, and crushed caraway seeds to saucepan. Sauté for 1–2 minutes.

Add tomatoes and water, bring to a boil. Reduce heat and simmer for 10 minutes. Add cabbage and beet greens to soup, and simmer for another 10 minutes.

Spoon 2 tablespoons of yogurt onto each serving and garnish with chives.

Per Serving		
	Calories: 96	% Fat Calories: 18%
	Saturated Fat: 0	Fiber: 4 grams
	Total Fat: 2 grams	Sodium: 480 mg

Borscht

Passover Kishke

Enjoy this flavorful kishke dish with all its trimmings for a Passover Seder. You can prepare the kishke roll in advance, and bake just before serving.

PREPARATION TIME: 50 MINUTES
BAKING TIME: 1 HOUR
SERVES: 8

4 Tbsp	**Virgin olive oil**
4 medium	**Celery stalks, diced**
4 medium	**Carrots, diced**
1 large	**Onion, diced**
1 tsp	**Sea salt**
1/4 tsp	**Ground pepper**
2 cups	**Italian parsley, chopped**
4 medium	**Garlic cloves, minced**
1 Tbsp	**Paprika**
4 cups	**Matzo meal**
2 cups	**Vegetable stock (see page 139)**
4 cups	**Spinach, large fresh leaves, stems removed, steamed**

Preheat oven to 350°F.

Heat a skillet over medium-high heat and add oil. Sauté celery, carrots, and onion with salt and black pepper 4–5 minutes. Add parsley, garlic, and paprika and heat 1 minute. Combine with matzo meal and stock. Mix well, and roll into two 12-inch long by 2-inch wide tubes. Wrap in aluminum foil. Bake 60 minutes.

Remove kishke from the oven. Remove foil and place on a serving platter. Cover kishke with lightly steamed spinach leaves.

To serve, slice rolls at an angle into 3–4 inch thick slices. Serve with gravy.

Apart from Passover, you can wrap these kishke rolls in fillo dough, making an elegant package. To make with fillo, cut 4 (12x17-inch) fillo sheets in half, forming 8 (12x8-inch) sheets. Layer 4 sheets on top of each other, with the best sheet on the bottom, spraying each layer for 2–3 seconds with virgin olive oil. Remove rolls after baking 40 minutes. Place kishke rolls at edge of fillo stacks and roll into cylinders. Bake an additional 20 minutes.

Per Serving			
	Calories: 379	% Fat Calories: 22%
	Saturated Fat: 1.4 grams	Fiber: 12 grams
	Total Fat: 10 grams	Sodium: 801 mg

Passover Gravy

PREPARATION TIME: 10 MINUTES
SIMMERING TIME: 20 MINUTES
SERVES: 8

1 Tbsp	**Virgin olive oil**
2 cups	**Mushrooms, sliced**
1 large	**Onion, diced**
2 medium	**Carrots, diced**
1/4 tsp	**Sea salt**
2 Tbsp	**Parsley, chopped**
1 1/2 cups	**Red wine**
1 1/4 cups	**Vegetable stock (see page 139)**

Heat sauté pan over medium-high heat and add oil. Sauté mushrooms, onion, carrots, salt, and parsley 5 minutes. Add red wine and vegetable stock. Reduce heat and simmer 20 minutes.

Purée ingredients in a blender. Add more liquid if too thick. Serve, drizzled over kishke.

Per Serving
Calories: 90
Saturated Fat: 0.4 grams
Total Fat: 2.6 grams
Fat Calories: 34%
Fiber: 1.5 grams
Sodium: 407 mg

Charoset

Spread on matzo crackers, and place on small plates around the table.

PREPARATION TIME: 10 MINUTES
SERVES: 8

1 1/3 cups	**Dates, pitted**
1/4 cup	**Walnuts, whole**
1/2 cup	**Almonds, whole**
1/4 cup	**Port wine**
1 Tbsp	**Honey**
1 Tbsp	**Vinegar**
1 medium	**Apple, peeled, cored, and diced**
8 regular	**Matzo crackers, unsalted**

Combine dates, nuts, wine, honey, and vinegar in a blender and purée into a paste. Mix in diced apple.

Spread on matzo crackers and serve on several small plates around the table.

Per Serving
Calories: 300
Saturated Fat: 0.7 grams
Total Fat: 7.4 grams
% Fat Calories: 22%
Fiber: 4.7 grams
Sodium: 0

Passover Meal

Turkish Salad

This is a colorful salad with salty and sweet flavors, reminding me of traveling and dining in the Middle East. I prefer mixing the sweet and salty flavors, combining all the dressing ingredients and refrigerating one hour prior to serving. If you want to savor the Mandarin sweetness, add the Mandarin orange slices just before serving.

PREPARATION TIME: 10 MINUTES
SERVES: 8

1 small	**Red onion, sliced thinly**
1/2 cup	**Mint, chopped**
1/3 cup	**Green olives, pitted and chopped**
1/2 tsp	**Ground coriander**
1 tsp	**Paprika**
1/4 tsp	**Sea salt**
1/8 tsp	**Ground black pepper**
22 oz	**Mandarin orange slices (if canned, rinsed)**
8 cups	**Mixed green and red leafed salad greens**

Combine red onion, mint, olives, coriander, paprika, salt, black pepper and Mandarin orange slices. Mix and refrigerate 1 hour prior to serving.

Rinse and drain mixed salad greens. Toss with half the prepared mixture. Serve on individual plates, then spoon remaining half over salad on each plate.

Per Serving	Calories: 83	% Fat Calories: 14%
	Saturated Fat: 0.2 grams	Fiber: 4.1 grams
	Total Fat: 1.4 grams	Sodium: 155 mg

Broccoli with Lemon Sauce

PREPARATION TIME: 10 MINUTES
BOILING TIME: 15 MINUTES
SERVES: 8

1 medium	**Russet potato, peeled & cut into 1/2-inch cubes**
2 medium	**Lemons, juiced**
1/8 tsp	**Sea salt**
4 cups	**Broccoli flowerets, sliced into long strips**

Bring a 1/2 cup of water to a boil, then add potato. Boil 15 minutes and drain, saving cooking water. Discard potato. Combine lemon juice, salt, and potato cooking water. Cook over medium heat for 2 minutes.

Steam broccoli until al dente, about 3–4 minutes. Remove from heat and serve. Drizzle lemon sauce over the broccoli.

Per Serving	Calories: 30	% Fat Calories: 7.5%
	Saturated Fat: 0	Fiber: 2.4 grams
	Total Fat: 0.4 grams	Sodium: 47 mg

Fruit Compôte

Enjoy this compôte by choosing your favorite fresh and dried fruits. Simmering brings the flavors together and thickens the sauce. I prefer the fruit lightly cooked. The longer you simmer the fruit, the softer and more pudding like it becomes.

PREPARATION TIME: 10 MINUTES
SIMMERING TIME: 1 HOUR
SERVES: 8

2 cups	**Apples, sliced**
1 cup	**Prunes, pitted and dried**
1 cup	**Cherries, dried (or raisins)**
1 cup	**Peaches, dried (or apricots)**
3 cups	**Apple cider**
1 medium	**Lime, juiced**
1/4 tsp	**Powdered ginger**
1/8 tsp	**Sea salt**
1 medium	**Cinnamon stick**
3 whole	**Cloves**
1/2 cup	**Port wine (or 1/2 cup extra apple cider)**
1/2 cup	**Nonfat yogurt (optional)**

Garnish:

1/4 cup	**Walnuts, roasted and chopped**
1 cup	**Fresh strawberries, sliced (or other fresh berries)**

Combine all ingredients except yogurt and garnishes in a large pot. Bring to a gentle boil, then simmer for 30-40 minutes. Remove the cinnamon stick and cloves.

Serve in individual bowls. Add 1–2 tablespoons of yogurt to each bowl.

Roast nuts for 6 minutes in the oven at 300°F, or microwave for 1 minute. Chop and sprinkle over bowls. Serve warm or chilled. Garnish with sliced strawberries.

Per Serving   Calories: 208   % Fat Calories: 12%
                Saturated Fat: 0.3 grams   Fiber: 3.3 grams
                Total Fat: 2.9 grams   Sodium: 50 mg

Easter Brunch

Easter represents the renewal of life. To me, Easter is a clear reminder to rekindle my energies toward spreading love and warmth. Invite friends or family for an Easter brunch, fill vases with flowers, and share love and kindness freely.

Easter Brunch Menu

Coffee or Tea

✤

Fresh Squeezed Orange Juice
with
Sparkling Cider or Champagne

✤

Crêpes with Fresh Spinach, Herbs & Yogurt

✤

Asparagus & Carrot Spears with Orange Vinaigrette

✤

Pineapple-Carrot Cake
or
Grapefruit Sorbet

Easter Brunch Preparation Plan

Plan for 2 1/2 hours of total preparation time. On a sunny day, aim to serve brunch outside. If the weather doesn't cooperate, surround your inside table with flowers. For a shopping list, see page 144.

DAY BEFORE PARTY (1 HOUR PREP TIME)
- Make crêpes. Wrap and refrigerate. They can be frozen for 1–2 weeks in advance. If making crêpes is new to you, consider making a double batch, and giving yourself extra time.
- Bake cake, wrap and refrigerate; or, prepare grapefruit sorbet.

Wrap crêpes and cake separately. Refrigerate or freeze.

BEFORE THE PARTY (1 HOUR PREP TIME)
- Preheat oven to 350°F. Set the table.
- Remove crêpes and cake from the refrigerator or freezer.
- Make crêpe filling, chop parsley garnish, and set aside.
- Fill crêpes.
- Make cake icing and garnish the cake on a serving plate.
- Prepare asparagus and carrot spears for steaming. Prepare the dressing.

20 MINUTES PRIOR TO SERVING THE MEAL
- Bake crêpes.
- 10 minutes prior to serving, steam asparagus and carrots.
- Garnish crêpes, mix asparagus and carrots with dressing, and serve.
- Mix orange juice with sparkling cider or champagne in a pitcher to serve with brunch. Add a slice of orange to each glass.

Crêpes with Fresh Spinach, Herbs & Yogurt

Crêpes are fun to make. This filling goes well with the asparagus orange-vinaigrette dish.

PREPARATION TIME: 45 MINUTES
SERVES: 6 (MAKES 12 CRÊPES)

Crêpes:

1 cup	Whole wheat pastry flour
1 cup	Nonfat milk (or soy milk plus 1/4 cup water)
1 tsp	Virgin olive oil
1/3 cup	Water
1/2 tsp	Sea salt
1 tsp	Italian herbs
3 large	Egg whites (or 2 Tbsp ground flax seed plus 3/4 cup water)
2 tsp	Virgin olive oil spray

Filling:

1 Tbsp	Virgin olive oil
1 medium	Onion, diced
2 cups	Mushrooms, sliced
1/2 tsp	Sea salt
1 tsp	Italian herbs, dried
1/4 cup	Vegetable stock
14 cups	Fresh spinach leaves, stemmed (a 6-ounce bag)
15 oz	White beans, cooked
1/2 cup	Nonfat yogurt (optional)
1/2 cup	Parmesan cheese, grated (or soy cheese)

Garnish:

1/2 cup	Parsley, chopped
1 medium	Orange, sliced

Preheat oven to 375°F.

Crêpes:
To make batter, whisk together milk, oil, water, salt, herbs, and egg whites. Combine with flour and mix well.

Heat a crêpe pan or a small 8-inch non-stick skillet over medium heat. Before adding crêpe batter, spray pan for one second with oil. Pour 1/8 cup of batter into the hot pan. Tip pan to spread the batter evenly. Cook crêpes until golden, about 20–30 seconds for each side. Set aside. Repeat process until you have made 12 crêpes. (The first 1–2 crêpes are the hardest, because they stick to an unevenly greased and heated pan.)

Filling:
Meanwhile, heat a sauté pan over medium-high heat. Add oil and sauté onion, mushrooms and salt for 3–4 minutes. Add herbs. Heat 1 minute, then add stock, spinach and white beans. Stir and heat 1 minute until spinach is limp but vividly green. Remove from heat and mix with yogurt.

Fill and roll crêpes with above mixture and place in an oven-proof pan. Sprinkle cheese over the crêpes. Bake 15–20 minutes. Garnish with parsley and orange slices, and serve.

Per Serving Calories: 312 % Fat Calories: 21.6%
Saturated Fat: 2.1 grams Fiber: 11 grams
Total Fat: 8.0 grams Sodium: 642 mg

Easter Brunch

Asparagus & Carrot Spears with Orange Vinaigrette

This is a lovely dish with fresh asparagus appearing in the market. I prefer thick asparagus spears for their flavor, and because they don't overcook so easily when steaming. Choose carrots with an equal diameter to the asparagus; carrots are more elegant with green tops still attached.

PREPARATION TIME: 10 MINUTES
SERVES: 6

24 large	Asparagus spears
18 small	Carrots with tops
12 baby	Yellow squash, or cubed yellow squash

Vinaigrette:

1/4 cup	Freshly squeezed orange juice
1/4 cup	Balsamic vinegar
1/2 tsp	Soy sauce, low-sodium
1 Tbsp	Extra virgin olive oil
1 tsp	Dijon mustard
1/2 tsp	Dried dill weed

Garnish:

| 1 medium | Orange, sliced into thin wedges |

Trim the base off asparagus spears, and trim carrot tops to 2 inches. Steam with squash until al dente. Remove from heat and dip in ice water to arrest cooking process. Drain and set aside.

Mix or whisk orange-vinaigrette ingredients until smooth.

To serve, combine asparagus, squash, and carrot spears with vinaigrette. Arrange spears on a serving plate. Garnish with orange wedges.

Per Serving	Calories: 108	% Fat Calories: 23%
	Saturated Fat: 0.4 grams	Fiber: 6 grams
	Total Fat: 2.7 grams	Sodium: 75 mg

Pineapple-Carrot Cake

This is an easy to make dessert, or it can be served as a great snack. Chop the nuts and dried fruit coarsely, leaving chewy pieces within the cake.

PREPARATION TIME: 15–20 MINUTES
BAKING TIME: 45–50 MINUTES
SERVES: 10

1 Tbsp	Canola oil
2 large	Egg whites
1 1/4 cups	Brown sugar
1 tsp	Vanilla extract
1 cup	Carrots, grated
4 oz	Pineapple chunks, chopped (1/2 cup)
1/2 cup	Pecans, coarsely chopped
1 cup	Dried fruit (raisins, apricots, peaches), coarsely chopped
1 1/2 cups	Whole wheat pastry flour
1 tsp	Baking powder
1/2 tsp	Sea salt
1 tsp	Cinnamon
1 tsp	Ground ginger

Glaze:

1/2 cup	Confectioner's (icing) sugar
2 Tbsp	Freshly squeezed lemon juice
1 medium	Lemon peel, grated
1/4 cup	Nonfat yogurt
8 slivers	Candied ginger

Preheat oven to 375°F.

Spray a 9x5x3-inch loaf pan with oil then dust with flour. In a bowl, mix oil, egg whites and sugar together. Add vanilla, carrots, pineapple, pecans, and dried fruit. Sift flour, baking powder, salt, cinnamon, and ginger together. Add liquid to dry ingredients, and mix to form batter.

Pour the batter into a greased loaf pan. Bake until an inserted toothpick comes out clean (45–50 minutes). Place on a rack 5–10 minutes. Remove pan and let cool on a rack.

For the glaze, sift confectioner's sugar into a bowl. Mix in lemon juice and yogurt. Once the cake has cooled, spread icing over the top of the cake, just to the edges. Grate lemon peel into thin long strips. Garnish cake with grated lemon zest and slivers of candied ginger.

Per Serving	Calories: 490	% Fat Calories: 18.5%
	Saturated Fat: 0.6 grams	Fiber: 3.2 grams
	Total Fat: 5.7 grams	Sodium: 172 mg

Pineapple-Carrot Cake

Grapefruit Sorbet

Easy-to-make and amazingly flavorful.

PREPARATION TIME: 15 MINUTES
FREEZING TIME: 10–15 MINUTES IN AN ICE CREAM MAKER / 6–10 HOURS IN THE FREEZER
SERVES: 6

3 cups	Grapefruit juice, fresh
2/3 cup	Sugar
4 Tbsp	Triple Sec liqueur (or 1 tsp orange extract)
3 Tbsp	Canola oil (or almond oil)
1 tsp	Lemon rind, grated

Garnish:

1 Tbsp	Lemon rind, grated
6 sprigs	Mint, fresh

Combine all ingredients in a blender and mix well. Process in an ice cream maker or freeze for at least 6 hours.

When ready to serve, scoop into individual bowls and garnish with lemon rind and mint.

Per Serving	Calories: 229	% Fat Calories: 30%
	Saturated Fat: 0.5 grams	Fiber: 0
	Total Fat: 6.9 grams	Sodium: 0

Cinco de Mayo Fiesta

Cinco de Mayo is a popular Mexican holiday celebrated widely across the United States. It celebrates Mexico's victory over the French invasion in Mexico in 1862. It also happens to be my son's birthday. In our home, we've learned to combine my wife's upbringing in Mexico with a birthday party. While the children celebrate with nachos, cake, Mexican hot chocolate and a piñata, this is what we might serve the adults.

Cinco de Mayo Fiesta Menu

Margaritas

❖

Guacamole with Jicama

❖

Seitan Enchiladas with Roasted Peppers

❖

Chiles Rellenos

❖

Black Beans

❖

Sweet Potato Flan

or

Fried Plantains with Banana Ice

Cinco de Mayo Fiesta Preparation Plan

Plan for 2–3 hours of total preparation time. I prepare the enchilada and chile relleno sauces, roast all the peppers, marinate the seitan, prepare the black beans, and make the flan the day before–not only does this give me more time for the party, but it also adds more flavor to the food. If you invite children, consider filling a piñata with healthy snacks. For a shopping list, see page 145.

1-2 DAYS BEFORE PARTY (1 1/2–2 HOURS PREP TIME)
- Prepare sauces for the enchiladas and the chiles rellenos.
- Marinate the seitan.
- Roast the peppers.
- Prepare the margarita mixture.
- Prepare black beans.
- Prepare and bake the flan; or, prepare plantains with banana ice.

Wrap or seal items in separate containers. Store in the refrigerator. Freeze the margarita mixture.

BEFORE THE PARTY (1 HOUR PREP TIME)
- Preheat oven to 350°F. Set the table.
- Prepare sauté stuffing for the enchiladas and the chiles rellenos.
- Prepare guacamole, place in a serving bowl and garnish. Slice the jicama, and return to the refrigerator.
- Assemble enchiladas and chiles rellenos.

20 MINUTES PRIOR TO SERVING THE MEAL
- Bake enchiladas and chiles rellenos.
- Heat black beans over low heat.
- Serve margaritas and guacamole with sliced jicama.

TO SERVE
- Dishes can be served buffet style, family style, or presented on individual plates.
- Garnish plates with sprigs of fresh cilantro.

Fried Plantains with Banana Ice

Margaritas

My father-in-law, a Frenchman, has spent much of his life in Mexico. Over the years he has learned several Margarita recipes. Here is my favorite. Caution: It is hard to notice the alcohol in this drink. Limit servings, especially to any potential drivers!

PREPARATION TIME: 10 MINUTES
MAKES: 5 CUPS (10 SERVINGS)

1 cup	**Freshly squeezed lime juice**
1 cup	**Tequila, clear**
1 1/3 cups	**Cointreau, or Triple Sec liqueur**
1/2 cup	**Sugar**
1 1/4 cups	**Water**
2 medium	**Limes, sliced**

Combine all ingredients in a blender, blend until smooth, then place in the freezer for at least 24 hours.

Slice a lime and rub the lime along the rim of a margarita glass. If you prefer a salted glass with your margarita, place 1/4 cup of coarse sea salt on a dessert plate. Invert the glass and dip the rim in salt.

Remove the margarita slush from the freezer and pour immediately into a prepared glass. Serve with a slice of lime.

Per Serving	Calories: 209	% Fat Calories: 0
	Saturated Fat: 0 grams	Fiber: 0
	Total Fat: 0 grams	Sodium: 0 grams

Limes

Guacamole with Jicama

This is a protein-enriched, reduced-fat version of guacamole. Serve with slices of jicama, drizzled with lime juice. Add a bowl of baked chips on the side.

PREPARATION TIME: 15 MINUTES
SERVES: 6

8 oz	**Garbanzo beans**
1 medium	**Avocado, peeled and mashed**
1/2 medium	**Onion, minced**
1 medium	**Garlic clove, minced**
1 medium	**Lime, juiced**
1/8 tsp	**Cayenne pepper**
1/4 tsp	**Sea salt**
1/8 tsp	**Cumin, ground**
1/4 cup	**Fresh cilantro, chopped**

Garnish:

Few	**Cilantro sprigs**
1 large	**Jicama, thinly sliced**
1 large	**Lime, juiced**
1 dash	**Paprika**
2 cups	**Baked chips**

Rinse, drain, and purée garbanzo beans. Combine mashed avocado with garbanzo beans. Add onion, garlic, lime juice, cayenne pepper, salt, cumin, and cilantro. Mix well. Place in a serving bowl and garnish with sprigs of cilantro.

Peel and slice jicama. Drizzle lime juice over slices. Sprinkle with paprika.

Per Serving

Calories: 157	% Fat Calories: 33%
Saturated Fat: 0.9 grams	Fiber: 4.5 grams
Total Fat: 6.3 grams	Sodium: 214 mg

Avocado

Chiles Rellenos

You can choose many types of peppers to stuff. I prefer poblano chiles, mild-to-very spicy. For tender palates, consider bell peppers without the "enchiloso" hot-spice.

PREPARATION TIME: 40 MINUTES
BAKING TIME: 20 MINUTES
SERVES: 6

6 medium	Poblano chiles
15 oz	Stewed tomatoes, canned
1 large	Red bell pepper, roasted and chopped (see page 138)
1/4 tsp	Ground cumin
1/4 tsp	Chili powder (vary to taste)
3/4 cup	Black beans, cooked
1 Tbsp	Virgin olive oil
1 small	Onion, diced
1/4 tsp	Sea salt
1/2 tsp	Oregano, dried
1/4 tsp	Ground cumin
3/4 cup	Corn kernels, fresh or frozen
2 medium	Tomatoes, chopped
1/4 cup	Cilantro, chopped

Garnish:

Few	Cilantro sprigs

Roast poblano chiles. See page 138. Gently remove the thin outer skin, keeping chiles intact. With a single slit lengthwise, open the chiles and remove seeds. Keep the stem on the chile. Set chiles aside.

Preheat oven to 350°F.

To prepare sauce, place stewed tomatoes, roasted red bell pepper, cumin, and chili powder in a blender. Purée until smooth. Pour in a saucepan and simmer 10 minutes to combine flavors. Set aside.

Rinse and drain cooked black beans. Set aside.

Heat a skillet over medium-high heat and add oil. Sauté onion and salt until the onion turns yellow, about 3 minutes. Add herbs, cumin, corn, and tomatoes. Cook for 2 minutes over medium heat, stirring occasionally. Add cilantro and cook for 30 seconds. Remove from heat.

Spoon 2 tablespoons of beans into each prepared chile. Divide the onion and corn mixture and spoon equally into each chile. Bake in an ovenproof casserole for 20 minutes.

To serve heat tomato and red bell pepper purée. Pour 1/6 of sauce on to each plate. Set baked chile on top of sauce. Garnish chiles with a sprig of cilantro.

Per Serving	Calories: 171	% Fat Calories: 26%
	Saturated Fat: 0.8 grams	Fiber: 5.8 grams
	Total Fat: 4.9 grams	Sodium: 507 mg

Seitan Enchiladas with Roasted Bell Peppers

This is a flavorful enchilada recipe featuring seitan (braised wheat gluten). Look for it in Oriental food stores. It adds a satisfying texture to the filling, and should be marinated 8–24 hours in advance. You could substitute black or pinto beans for seitan.

PREPARATION TIME: 30 MINUTES
BAKING TIME: 20 MINUTES
SERVES: 6

Filling:

15 oz	Seitan
2 medium	Garlic cloves, chopped
1/2 tsp	Cumin, ground
1 tsp	Soy sauce, low-sodium
1/4 tsp	Cayenne pepper
3/4 cup	Tomato sauce (6 oz)
1 medium	Red bell pepper
1/2 cup	Non-fat Monterey Jack (or soy cheese), grated
1/4 cup	Pecans, chopped

Sauce:

2 tsp	Virgin olive oil
1 medium	Onion, diced
1 tsp	Oregano, dried
1 tsp	Crushed red pepper
1/2 tsp	Ground cumin
15 oz	Stewed tomatoes, puréed
15 oz	Tomato sauce
4 medium	Garlic cloves, chopped
1 cup	Corn kernels (8 oz)
1/4 cup	Cilantro, chopped
1 large	Tomato, chopped
2 medium	Red bell peppers, roasted and chopped

Wrapping:

12 medium	Corn tortillas
1 cup	Lowfat Monterey Jack (or soy cheese), grated

Garnish:

1/4 cup	Cilantro sprigs
1/2 medium	Roasted pepper, thinly sliced

Roast peppers and chop. (See page 138)

Filling:
Drain seitan and combine with garlic, cumin, soy sauce, cayenne pepper, tomato sauce, and 1 chopped, roasted pepper. Marinate overnight, or at least 8 hours.

Preheat oven to 350°F.

Sauce:
Heat a large sauce pan over medium-high heat and add oil. Sauté onion for 2–3 minutes. Add oregano, crushed red pepper, and cumin. Cook 1 minute. Add stewed tomatoes, tomato sauce, and garlic. Cook 2–3 minutes. Place in a blender or food processor and process until smooth. Return to sauce pan. Add corn, cilantro, tomato and roasted bell peppers and simmer over low heat for 10 minutes.

Wrapping:
Dip tortillas in the sauce for 1–2 minutes. Combine marinated seitan with cheese and chopped pecans. Divide filling into each dipped tortilla and roll it like a burrito.

Pour half the sauce into a 9x12-inch ovenproof dish, and arrange rolled tortillas on it. Pour remaining sauce over enchiladas and sprinkle cheese on top. Bake 20 minutes.

Garnish:
Garnish with sprigs of cilantro and roasted bell pepper strips.

Per Serving	Calories: 456	% Fat Calories: 22%
	Saturated Fat: 1.7 grams	Fiber: 7.5 grams
	Total Fat: 12 grams	Sodium: 1000 mg

Black Beans

PREPARATION TIME: 10 MINUTES
SERVES: 6

15 ounces	**Black beans, cooked and rinsed**
2 cloves	**Garlic, minced**
1/2 cup	**Tomato salsa**
Garnish:	
Few	**Cilantro sprigs**
Few	**Bell pepper strips**

Heat beans and garlic in a pan until gently bubbling. Add salsa, stir, and remove from heat.

Place beans in a serving dish and garnish with sprigs of cilantro and strips of bell pepper.

Per Serving   Calories: 108   % Fat Calories: 4%
Saturated Fat: 0 grams   Fiber: 7 grams
Total Fat: 0.5 grams   Sodium: 118 mg

Cinco de Mayo Fiesta Meal

Sweet Potato Flan

Here is an easy-to-make, delicious dessert, low in fat, and full of antioxidants. What a deal! Great served with Mexican hot chocolate.

PREPARATION TIME: 25 MINUTES
BAKING TIME: 60 MINUTES
SERVES: 6–8

Filling:

1 small	Sweet potato, cooked, peeled and mashed (1 cup)
6 large	Egg whites
14 oz	Sweet condensed nonfat milk
14 oz	Water
1 tsp	Vanilla extract
1 Tbsp	Orange peel, grated
3 Tbsp	Almond oil (or canola oil)

Caramel:

1/3 cup	Sugar
1/4 cup	Water

Garnish:

1 cup	Fresh berries
Few	Sprigs fresh mint

Preheat oven to 275°F.

Fill a 9x13-inch baking dish with 2 cups of water (about 1/3 full). Place in the oven.

Prick the sweet potato with a fork. Microwave 8–10 minutes, until soft (or bake 30–40 minutes). Cut sweet potato in half and scoop out the pulp. Discard the skin.

Place egg whites, milk, water, sweet potato pulp, vanilla, orange peel, and oil in a blender and purée until smooth.

Caramel:
Combine water and sugar in a saucepan. Cook over high heat. Do not stir. Boil 5–6 minutes until golden brown. Remove syrup from heat immediately. Pour equal amounts of syrup into individual pudding dishes, or a soufflé dish.

Pour sweet potato-milk purée over caramel in pudding dishes or soufflé dish. Carefully transfer into the baking dish with water (hot water bath). Bake for 1 1/2 hours. (Cooking longer increases firmness but decreases smoothness.) Set aside to cool. Refrigerate.

To serve, slide a knife along the edges of the flan dish(es). Invert dish(es) onto dessert plate(s). Garnish with fresh berries and a sprig of fresh mint.

Per Serving	Calories: 215	% Fat Calories: 29%
	Saturated Fat: 0.6 grams	Fiber: 2 grams
	Total Fat: 7 grams	Sodium: 87 mg

Fried Plantains with Banana Ice

Fried plantains are a popular dessert in Mexico and many other Hispanic countries. They are delightful over this dairy-free ice cream.

PREPARATION TIME: 20 MINUTES
FREEZING TIME: 10–15 MINUTES IN AN ICE CREAM MAKER, OR 6–10 HOURS IN THE FREEZER
SERVES: 6

Banana Ice:

1 large	Banana, ripe, peeled
2 cups	Rice milk
1/3 cup	Maple syrup
2 Tbsp	Dark rum (or 1 tsp vanilla extract)
3 Tbsp	Lime juice, freshly squeezed
1/8 tsp	Sea salt

Fried plantains:

2 Tbsp	Canola oil
3 small	Plantains (or bananas)
1/8 tsp	Cinnamon

Garnish:

6 sprigs	Mint, fresh

Banana Ice:
Combine banana ice ingredients in a blender and mix well. Process mixture in an ice cream maker or place in the freezer for at least 6 hours.

Fried Plantains:
Peel and slice plantains lengthwise into 1/4-inch thick slices.

In a non-stick skillet, heat 1 tablespoon of oil. Spread half of the sliced plantains on the hot skillet. Sauté until the bottoms brown nicely. Turn and brown the other side. Remove plantains from pan and sprinkle a dash of cinnamon over them. Repeat this process with the second batch of plantains.

When ready to serve, scoop banana ice into individual bowls and top it with the fried plantains. Garnish with a sprig of fresh mint.

Per Serving	Calories: 270	Fiber: 4 grams
	Saturated Fat: 0.4 grams	%Fat Calories: 17%
	Total Fat: 4.4 grams	Sodium: 56 mg

Fourth of July Celebration

These dishes are colorful and delicious, featuring reds, whites, and blues. Decorate the lasagna with stars and stripes to make the dinner an especially patriotic celebration. Enjoy dessert while watching the fireworks!

Fourth of July Celebration Menu

Red, White, & Blue Fruit Punch

✣

Spicy Asparagus Dip

✣

Gazpacho

✣

Stars & Stripes Lasagna

✣

Tomato-Cauliflower Salad with Blueberry Vinaigrette

✣

Blueberry & Strawberry Crumble

Fourth of July Preparation Plan

Plan for 2 1/2–3 hours of total preparation time. For a shopping list, see page 146.

DAY BEFORE PARTY (1 1/2 HOURS PREP TIME)
- Prepare tomato sauce.
- Make lasagna.
- Cover lasagna with foil and refrigerate.

BEFORE THE PARTY (2 HOURS PREP TIME)
- Preheat oven to 375°F.
- Prepare gazpacho. Refrigerate in a serving bowl.
- Make punch and refrigerate.
- Prepare asparagus dip. Refrigerate in a serving bowl.
- Prepare salad. Refrigerate, keeping salad and dressing apart until ready to serve.
- For the berry crumble: combine ingredients in a saucepan, heat, then pour into a pie plate and refrigerate.
- Toast granola and almonds in a sauté pan and set aside separately.

20 MINUTES PRIOR TO SERVING
- Bake lasagna.
- Serve punch and asparagus dip.
- Toss salad with dressing.

TO SERVE
- Remove lasagna from the oven.
- Serve gazpacho soup.
- Just before serving the lasagna and salad, place crumble in the oven at 375°F. Set the timer for 20 minutes.
- To serve the crumble, reheat granola and almonds for 1–2 minutes. Sprinkle granola and almonds over the baked fruit. Spoon onto individual plates, and garnish with fresh berries and sprigs of mint.

Asparagus

Red, White, & Blue Fruit Punch

PREPARATION TIME: 10–15 MINUTES
SERVES: 8

4 cups	Seltzer
4 cups	Grape juice
2 cups	Strawberries, thinly sliced
2 cups	Fresh blueberries
1 small	Jicama, peeled and cut into 1/2-inch cubes

Combine ingredients. Serve in cups. Provide spoons for the fruit.

Per Serving Calories: 114 % Fat Calories: 3%
Saturated Fat: 0 grams Fiber: 2.7 grams
Total Fat: 0.4 grams Sodium: 0 mg

Spicy Asparagus Dip

Here is a lovely dip with holiday colors. Serve with vegetable sticks, pita bread triangles, or jicama slices.

PREPARATION TIME: 15 MINUTES
MAKES: ABOUT 3 CUPS
SERVES: 8

1 lb	Asparagus spears
3 Tbsp	Nonfat yogurt (optional)
2 Tbsp	Lemon juice
1/2 tsp	Cumin powder
1 medium	Garlic clove, minced
1/2 tsp	Italian herbs, dried
1/4 tsp	Cayenne pepper
1/4 tsp	Sea salt
1 medium	Tomato, chopped
1/2 cup	Parsley, finely chopped

Garnish:

Few	Parsley sprigs
1–2 dashes	Paprika

Trim off base of asparagus spears, and steam until al dente. Dip briefly in ice water to arrest cooking.

Meanwhile, place yogurt, lemon juice, cumin, garlic, Italian herbs, pepper, and salt in a blender and purée until smooth. Add steamed asparagus and blend.

Spoon asparagus dip into a serving bowl. Stir in chopped tomatoes and parsley. Garnish with sprigs of parsley and a dash of paprika.

Per Serving Calories: 32 % Fat Calories: 9%
Saturated Fat: 0 grams Fiber: 1.8 grams
Total Fat: 0.4 grams Sodium: 90 mg

Gazpacho

Vine-ripened tomatoes and fresh herbs form a delicious, cold, summer soup. You could also serve this as a meal on any summer day with a green salad and whole grain bread.

PREPARATION: 15 MINUTES
CHILL: 15–30 MINUTES
SERVES: 8

1/2 tsp	**Virgin olive oil**
6 medium	**Garlic cloves, diced**
1 large	**Red bell pepper, chopped**
1/2 tsp	**Ground cumin**
1/2 tsp	**Paprika**
1/2 tsp	**Sea salt**
4 medium	**Vine-ripened tomatoes**
1 slice	**Whole wheat bread, toasted and crumbled (1/2 cup)**
1 medium	**Lemon, juiced**
1/4 cup	**Parsley, fresh**
1/4 cup	**Basil, fresh**
1/4 cup	**Mint leaves, fresh**
1 cup	**Cold water**
2 Tbsp	**Balsamic vinegar**
1 medium	**Cucumber, peeled and chopped**
Garnish:	
1/4 cup	**Fresh herbs**

Heat a sauté pan over medium heat and add oil. Add garlic, chopped pepper, cumin, paprika, and salt and sauté for 2 minutes. Remove from heat and set aside.

Place tomatoes, bread, lemon juice, herbs, water, and vinegar in a blender and purée. Add the sauté mixture and cucumber.

Pulse briefly, leaving bits of red pepper and cucumber. Chill for 15–30 minutes.

Pour into individual bowls and garnish with fresh herbs.

Per Serving	Calories: 81	% Fat Calories: 18%
	Saturated Fat: 0.3 grams	Fiber: 2 grams
	Total Fat: 2 grams	Sodium: 230 mg

Stars & Stripes Lasagna

This dish is a big hit on the Fourth of July. Ask your store in advance for star-shaped pasta, or cook lasagna noodles and cut them into star shapes with a knife or a star-shaped cookie cutter.

PREPARATION TIME: 40 MINUTES (PLUS TIME TO PREPARE SAUCE)
BAKING TIME: 20 MINUTES
SERVES: 8–10

3 cups	Tomato sauce (prepared, or see recipe next page)
9 medium	Spinach lasagna noodles
1/4 cup	Star-shaped pasta

Cheese layer:

6 oz	Mozzarella, nonfat, grated
6 oz	Mozzarella, part skim, grated

Spinach layer:

9 cups	Fresh spinach leaves, or
	(2) 10-oz packs frozen spinach
2 cups	Green beans
4 medium	Garlic cloves, minced
1 cup	Parsley, chopped
1 Tbsp	Virgin olive oil

White sauce:

3 Tbsp	Virgin olive oil
1 small	White onion, minced
3 Tbsp	All purpose flour
1/3 cup	Nonfat milk
2 oz	Mozzarella, nonfat, grated
2 oz	Mozzarella, part skim, grated
6 Tbsp	Parmesan cheese, grated

Preheat oven to 375°F.

Bring water to a boil. Cook lasagna noodles until al dente, about 12 minutes. (I'll usually cook 12 noodles and pick the best 9 noodles for lasagna layers.) Drain, rinse with cold water, and set aside. Cook star shaped pasta (or white lasagna cut into stars if you can't find star shaped pasta) until al dente. Drain, rinse with cold water, and set aside.

Spinach layer:
Steam spinach and green beans about 3 minutes. Drain out remaining liquid. Sauté garlic and parsley in oil for 1 minute. Combine with spinach and green beans. Set aside.

White sauce:
Heat a saucepan with oil, sauté the onion until soft and translucent. Add flour and stir, heating 30 seconds. Add milk. When it bubbles, simmer for 2–3 minutes. Add the cheeses, stir until smooth. Remove from heat. Set aside.

In a 9x13-inch baking dish, build lasagna layers with 3 lasagna noodles on the bottom, a spinach layer with 1/2 of the spinach and green beans, then a layer with 1/3 of the tomato sauce, and a cheese layer with 1/2 of the grated cheeses. Repeat layering sequence for the second layer. Cover with a third layer of lasagna noodles.

To decorate the top level in the shape of the American flag, arrange star-shaped pasta in the top left corner. Pour white sauce and remaining tomato sauce into 1 1/2-inch stripes along the length of the baking pan, excluding the top left corner. Spray the pasta in the top-left corner with olive oil spray. Bake for 20 minutes. (See photo page 94.)

Vegan Option:

Rinse and drain 16 ounces of firm tofu. Slice into 1/4-inch slices. Spread on a non-stick baking dish. Season with a little olive oil, oregano, minced garlic, salt and pepper to taste. Bake in the pre-heated oven for 15 minutes. Set aside.

When assembling lasagna, substitute sliced, seasoned tofu for the cheese layers. For white sauce, substitute 1 cup of soy milk in place of 1/3 cup of milk and cheeses.

Per Serving	Calories: 557	% Fat Calories: 23%
	Saturated Fat: 4.4 grams	Fiber: 7 grams
	Total Fat: 14 grams	Sodium: 381 mg

Roasted Tomato Sauce with Tofu

Serve this sauce with pasta or use it in a casserole. The sauce freezes very well, and saves you precious preparation time later. If you like your tomatoes without the skin, dip them in boiling water for 1–2 minutes and the skins peel away easily. In July and August, when beautiful, vine-ripened tomatoes are plentiful, pack your freezer with roasted tomato sauce; you'll be glad all winter.

PREPARATION TIME: 15 MINUTES
ROASTING TIME: 30 MINUTES
SIMMERING TIME: 15–20 MINUTES
SERVES: 8 (4 CUPS)

8 medium	Vine-ripened tomatoes, peeled
1 tsp	Virgin olive oil
1 medium	Onion, chopped
1/2 tsp	Sea salt
1 tsp	Italian herbs, dried
3 Tbsp	Fresh basil, or 1 Tbsp dried
6 medium	Garlic cloves, chopped
2/3 cup	Red wine
2 cups	Mushrooms, sliced
1/2 lb	Tofu, firm, cut into 1/2-inch cubes

Preheat oven to 350°F.

To skin tomatoes, dip in boiling water for 1 minute. Set aside to cool. Peel.

Heat sauté pan over medium-high heat. Add oil. Sauté onions, salt, and herbs until onion is soft, 3–4 minutes. Add garlic and basil. Heat 1 minute. Place in a bowl and set aside. Sauté mushrooms in the same pan until tender, but still firm. Set aside.

Slice tomatoes and place in an baking dish. Add sautéed onion and herbs. Roast in the oven, stirring occasionally. As sauce begins to thicken (about 30 minutes), add red wine. Pour sauce in a blender, and purée until smooth. Pour into a sauce pan. Add mushrooms and tofu. Simmer until the sauce has thickened, about 15–20 minutes. Enjoy the sauce with lasagna or spaghetti.

Per Serving	Calories: 98	% Fat Calories: 33%
	Saturated Fat: 0.5 grams	Fiber: 2.5 grams
	Total Fat: 3.6 grams	Sodium: 203 mg

Tomato-Cauliflower Salad with Blueberry Vinaigrette

Add this lovely salad to your Fourth of July holiday party.

PREPARATION TIME: 20 MINUTES
SERVES: 8

1 medium	**Cauliflower, sliced**
12 medium	**Vine-ripened tomatoes, sliced thinly**
1 medium	**Red bell pepper, sliced thinly**
1 cup	**Parsley, finely chopped**

Blueberry Vinaigrette:

4 Tbsp	**Balsamic vinegar**
2 Tbsp	**Lemon juice**
1 tsp	**Dill weed**
1 1/2 Tbsp	**Extra virgin olive oil**
1 tsp	**Soy sauce, low-sodium**
1/2 cup	**Blueberries (fresh or frozen)**

Boil a pot of water. Blanch cauliflower for 3 minutes, then put in ice water for 5 minutes to arrest cooking process. Drain.

Combine cauliflower, tomatoes, bell pepper, and parsley. Put dressing ingredients in a blender, and mix until smooth. Toss with salad when ready to serve.

Per Serving Calories: 95   % Fat Calories: 29%
Saturated Fat: 0.4 grams   Fiber: 4 grams
Total Fat: 3.6 grams   Sodium: 75 mg

Stars & Stripes Lasagna

Blueberry & Strawberry Crumble

Blueberry & Strawberry Crumble

This delicious dessert is easy to make. Substitute fruit as desired. You can also serve this with a special brunch.

PREPARATION TIME: 10 MINUTES
BAKING TIME: 20 MINUTES
SERVES: 8

1/4 cup	Water
1/4 cup	Maple syrup
2 cups	Apples, cored and cut in 1/2-inch slices
1/4 tsp	Cinnamon, ground
2 Tbsp	Tapioca, quick cooking
2 cups	Blueberries, frozen or fresh
2 cups	Strawberries, frozen or fresh
1 medium	Lime, juiced
1 1/2 cups	Low-fat granola (No more than 30% of calories from fat)
1/4 cup	Almonds, sliced

Garnish:

1/4 cup	Mixed fresh berries
Few	Mint sprigs

Preheat oven to 375°F.

In a saucepan, combine water, maple syrup, apples, cinnamon, and tapioca. Bring to a boil. Lower heat and simmer for 5 minutes.

Add berries and lime juice to tapioca-apple mixture. Mix well. Pour into a pie dish. Bake 20 minutes.

Meanwhile, toast the granola and almonds over medium-high heat for 4–5 minutes stirring frequently. Sprinkle granola and almonds over baked fruit just before you serve the crumble.

To serve, spoon onto plates and garnish with fresh berries and a sprig of mint.

Per Serving

Calories: 140	% Fat Calories: 18%
Saturated Fat: 0.3 grams	Fiber: 4.2 grams
Total Fat: 3.0 grams	Sodium: 5 mg

Summer Brunch

On a leisurely summer morning, enjoy brunch outside in the garden. You can make most of this meal the day before, with final touches before your guests arrive. Choose a lovely spot on the deck, patio, or garden for the table and meal. Decorate the table with fresh flowers.

Summer Brunch Menu

Sparkling Cider

✤

Vine-Ripened Tomatoes, Basil & Hearts of Palm Salad

✤

Mushroom Ragout with Risotto

✤

Mixed Green Salad with Mustard Vinaigrette

✤

Fruit Compôte Tarte
with
Tea or Coffee

Summer Brunch Preparation Plan

Plan for 3 1/2 hours of total preparation time. I like to make the mushroom ragout, risotto, and pie crust the day before the party. For a shopping list, see page 147.

DAY BEFORE PARTY (2 HOURS PREP TIME)
- Prepare mushroom ragout. Pour into a container and refrigerate.
- Make risotto. When it is nearly done, but still too chewy to serve, remove from heat, pour into a chilled cookie sheet, and place in the refrigerator immediately. Save one cup of stock for final cooking. Cover the cookie sheet with plastic wrap once the risotto has chilled.
- Prepare tarte dough, cover with plastic wrap, and refrigerate.

1 1/2 HOURS BEFORE THE PARTY
- Preheat oven to 400°F. Prepare compôte filling.
- Roll out tarte dough, and bake as directed.
- Decorate the table and place cider in the refrigerator.
- Heat mushroom ragout over low heat. Add stock if it appears too thick.
- Prepare both salads, place in serving bowls, and refrigerate. Store the salad dressings in separate containers until ready to toss into salad.

10 MINUTES PRIOR TO SERVING
- Place risotto in a saucepan. Warm over medium heat. Add stock 1/2 cup at a time while stirring. Add wine. Stir. When risotto is al dente, place in a serving dish, spoon mushroom ragout over the risotto, and garnish.

TO SERVE
- Toss salads with dressing and serve in respective serving dishes.
- Serve garnished risotto with ragout.

Vine-Ripened Tomatoes, Basil & Hearts of Palm Salad

I've enjoyed this simple salad many times. Choose the best quality tomatoes, balsamic vinegar and extra virgin olive oil for this salad.

PREPARATION TIME: 10 MINUTES
SERVES: 8

Garlic Vinaigrette:

3 Tbsp	**Balsamic vinegar**
1/4 tsp	**Dijon mustard**
1 medium	**Garlic clove minced**
1/2 tsp	**Soy sauce, low-sodium**
1/8 tsp	**Ground black pepper**
1/2 tsp	**Dill weed**

Salad:

6 medium	**Vine-ripened tomatoes, cut into 1/2-inch slices (or 4 cups vine-ripened cherry tomatoes, halved)**
30 oz	**Hearts of palm, drained and sliced**
1/2 cup	**Fresh basil, coarsely chopped**
1/3 cup	**Goat cheese (optional)**
1 1/2 Tbsp	**Extra virgin olive oil**

Whisk together vinegar, mustard, garlic, soy sauce, black pepper, and dill weed to make vinaigrette.

Arrange sliced tomatoes and hearts of palm on serving plates. Garnish plates with chopped basil. Drizzle dressing over salad.

Sprinkle goat cheese over each plate. (You can substitute grated parmesan for the goat cheese, or skip adding cheese entirely.)

Drizzle 1 teaspoon of your favorite extra virgin olive oil over each serving plate. Serve immediately.

Per Serving Calories: 186 % Fat Calories: 21%
Saturated Fat: 1.6 grams Fiber: 4.9 grams
Total Fat: 4.9 grams Sodium: 53 mg

Vine-Ripened Tomatoes, Basil & Hearts of Palm Salad

Mushroom Ragout with Risotto

I enjoy this dish with a variety of wild mushrooms—chanterelles, porcini, and morels being my favorites. Oyster and shiitake mushrooms work well, too. You can also use dried mushrooms. Soak them in very hot water for twenty minutes. Drain and reserve the liquid for the stock.

PREPARATION TIME: 1 HOUR
SIMMERING TIME: 20 MINUTES
SERVES: 8

Ragout:

1 Tbsp	Virgin olive oil
1 medium	Sweet onion, chopped
1/2 tsp	Sea salt
8 cups	Wild mushrooms (a mixture), sliced
1 tsp	Italian herbs, dried
1/4 tsp	Freshly ground black pepper
4 medium	Vine-ripened tomatoes, chopped
6 medium	Garlic cloves, minced
1/4 cup	Fresh basil, chopped
1 cup	Tomato sauce
1/2 cup	Red wine

Risotto:

2 medium	Leeks
2 Tbsp	Virgin olive oil
3 medium	Scallions, diced
2 cups	Arborio rice
6 cups	Vegetable stock
1 cup	White wine
1/4 cup	Parsley, finely chopped
2 Tbsp	Parmesan cheese (or soy), grated

Garnish:

1/4 cup	Parsley, chopped
2 Tbsp	Parmesan cheese (or soy), grated

Ragout:

Heat sauté pan over medium-high heat and add oil. Sauté onion with salt 2–3 minutes. Add mushrooms, herbs and pepper, sauté 2–3 minutes, stirring occasionally. Add tomatoes and garlic, cook 2–3 minutes. Add basil, tomato sauce, and wine. Reduce heat and simmer 20 minutes uncovered.

Risotto:

Meanwhile, slice leeks, discarding tiny bottom roots and green tops 1-inch above the white stem. Heat sauté pan over medium-high heat and add oil. Sauté leeks for 3–4 minutes. Add scallions, heat 1 minute. Add arborio rice. Heat 2 minutes, stirring frequently. Slowly add stock, 1/2 cup at a time, letting rice absorb stock. When all of the stock has absorbed, add white wine, 1/2 cup at a time. Stir continuously. When rice is al dente, stir in 2 tablespoons of grated cheese.

To serve, spoon rice on a plate, cover with mushroom ragout. Garnish with parsley and grated cheese.

Per Serving

Calories: 650	% Fat Calories: 14%
Saturated Fat: 2 grams	Fiber: 13 grams
Total Fat: 10 grams	Sodium: 1000 mg

Mixed Green Salad with Mustard Vinaigrette

Simple to make, and a nice accompaniment to the mushroom ragout.

PREPARATION TIME: 5 MINUTES
SERVES: 8

Salad:

8 cups	Mixed salad greens (preferably with several green and red varieties)
18 medium	Cherry tomatoes

Mustard Vinaigrette:

3 Tbsp	Balsamic vinegar
1 Tbsp	Wine, red
1/2 medium	Lemon, juiced
1 tsp	Soy sauce, low-sodium
1/2 tsp	Dijon mustard
1 dash	Black pepper, ground
1 Tbsp	Extra virgin olive oil (optional)

Garnish:

12 fresh	Edible flowers (if available)

Mix salad greens in a salad bowl. Cut tomatoes in half. Set aside in a separate dish.

Combine vinaigrette ingredients, and whisk until smooth. Toss greens and sliced tomatoes with vinaigrette. Garnish salad with flowers and serve.

Per Serving   Calories: 160   % Fat Calories: 21%
Saturated Fat: 0.6 grams   Fiber: 8.7 grams
Total Fat: 4.3 grams   Sodium: 116 mg

Mixed Green Salad with Mustard Vinaigrette

Fruit Compôte Tarte

Summer provides wonderful flavors for pies. You can substitute peaches for plums, and almost any berry for blueberries.

PREPARATION TIME: 1 HOUR
PIE DOUGH CHILLING TIME: 1–24 HOURS
BAKING TIME: 30–40 MINUTES
SERVES: 10 (MAKES ONE 9-INCH PIE)

Crust:

1 1/4 cups	Whole wheat pastry flour
3/4 cup	All purpose flour
1/2 tsp	Sea salt
1/2 cup	Chilled canola oil
5–6 Tbsp	Water, ice cold
1/4 tsp	Sugar
1/8 tsp	Cinnamon

Filling:

3 medium	Baking apples, cored and sliced
1/2 cup	Sugar
1/3 cup	Port wine
1 medium	Lime, juiced
1/4 tsp	Powdered ginger
1/4 cup	Tapioca, quick cooking
10 small	Plums, pitted and sliced
1 1/2 cups	Blueberries

Garnish:

1/2 cup	Fresh blueberries
2 Tbsp	Candied Ginger, thinly sliced

Crust:

Combine dry ingredients. Add chilled canola oil. Blend with a fork or pastry blender until it has the consistency of cornmeal with pea sized lumps. Handle gently, and don't over mix or the dough becomes tough. Sprinkle dough with water, 1 tablespoon at a time, adding just enough water to be able to form dough into a ball. Wrap dough in plastic wrap and refrigerate 1–24 hours. Place dough at room temperature 30 minutes before rolling. Save 1/4 of the dough for latticed pie cover.

Preheat oven to 400°F. Between 2 layers of wax paper, press dough into a flat circle. Roll dough from the center out, until it's about 1/8-inch thick and 2 inches wider than the pie dish. Patch tears, but avoid re-rolling dough. Spray dish lightly with canola oil. Ease dough into a 9-inch pie dish. Trim border and pinch edges. Cover pie dish and crust with foil. Fill dish with dried beans, bake 10–15 minutes. Remove beans and foil. Set aside to cool.

Filling:

Combine apples, sugar, port, lime juice, ginger, and tapioca. Heat in a pan over medium heat until just bubbling. Stir in plums and blueberries. Gently pour into pre-baked pie shell. Roll out remaining dough. Cut into 3/4-inch strips for lattice cover. Sprinkle strips with sugar and cinnamon. Cover pie with lattice strips.

Bake at 400°F for 10 minutes. Reduce heat to 350°F and bake another 25–35 minutes. Don't over-brown the pie crust. Set aside to cool for at least 1 hour. When serving, garnish plates with fresh berries and sliced candied ginger.

Per Serving	Calories: 331	% Fat Calories: 32%
	Saturated Fat: 0.9 grams	Fiber: 5.0 grams
	Total Fat: 12 grams	Sodium: 97 mg

Fall Equinox

Fall is a great time for a dinner party. Red, yellow, and golden leaves decorate the countryside. Homes grow cozy when it gets cooler outside. Light candles, warm up the house, and enjoy a dinner party.

Fall Equinox Party Menu

Butternut Squash Soup with Ginger & Fennel

✢

Red Pepper & Shiitake Polenta
with
Roasted Vegetables

✢

Mixed Greens Salad

✢

Pumpkin Pie

Fall Equinox Party Preparation Plan

Schedule 3 1/2 hours of total preparation time. I like to make the soup, polenta, and pumpkin pie the day before the party. For the party, I enjoy illuminating the house with candles and making a fire in the fireplace. For a shopping list, see page 147.

1–2 DAYS BEFORE THE PARTY (2 HOURS PREP TIME)
- Make butternut squash soup. Pour into a container, seal, and refrigerate.
- Prepare polenta. After baking in the oven, let cool, wrap polenta in the same cookie sheet and store in the refrigerator.
- Make and bake pumpkin pie. Let cool, cover and refrigerate.

1 1/2 HOURS BEFORE THE PARTY
- Prepare salad and salad dressing. Refrigerate. Keep dressing separate until ready to toss salad and serve.
- Cook polenta in the oven for 15 minutes at 250°F.
- Set oven to 350°F. Clean and slice vegetables to be roasted. Roast vegetables with herbs, salt, pepper, and virgin olive oil in the oven 30 minutes prior to serving.
- Cut polenta into 4-inch squares. Cut squares diagonally in half, forming triangles.
- Heat sauté pan(s), spray with virgin olive oil. Sauté polenta triangles on each side until golden. When all the polenta triangles are sautéed, transfer back to the oven to keep warm.
- Meanwhile, sauté leeks, green beans, garbanzo beans, and herbs. When they are nearly done, mix in with the roasting vegetables in the oven.
- Chop parsley for the polenta garnish and set aside.
- Heat soup over medium-low heat. Prepare fennel leave garnishes for the soup, and set aside.

TO SERVE
- When the roasting vegetables are almost al dente, turn off the oven, and enjoy soup. Don't over bake the vegetables.
- Transfer 2 polenta triangles onto each plate. Spoon vegetables over the polenta. Garnish with parsley.
- Serve with tossed salad.

Butternut Squash Soup with Ginger & Fennel

This is a fragrant soup for special occasions, or when you want a treat on a cool fall day.

PREPARATION TIME: 20 MINUTES
BAKING TIME: 30–40 MINUTES
SIMMERING TIME: 15 MINUTES
SERVES: 6–8

1 medium	**Butternut squash, baked**
2 tsp	**Canola oil**
1 medium	**Onion, diced**
1 tsp	**Sea salt**
1 Tbsp	**Ginger root, grated**
1/2 tsp	**Curry powder**
1/4 tsp	**Cumin powder**
1 cup	**Fennel root, chopped**
1/4 cup	**White wine**
2 cups	**Nonfat milk, or soy milk**
1 cup	**Vegetable stock (see page 139)**
2 Tbsp	**Maple syrup**

Garnish:

1/2 cup	**Sprigs fennel leaves**

Preheat oven to 350°F.

Cut squash in half, scoop out seeds, bake face down for 30–40 minutes, until soft.

Heat a skillet over medium-high heat and add oil. Sauté onion with salt until onion is soft, about 2 minutes.

Add ginger, curry, cumin powder, and fennel. Heat 2 minutes, stirring occasionally. Stir in wine, heat 30 seconds. Add milk, stock, and maple syrup. Stir and remove from heat. Purée in a blender.

Scoop squash pulp from its skin and add to puréed ingredients. Process in the blender until smooth, 1–2 minutes. Return to a saucepan and simmer 15 minutes.

To serve, garnish with fennel leaves. Optionally, garnish with a swirl of yogurt.

Per Serving	Calories: 145	% Fat Calories: 14.8%
	Saturated Fat: 0.4 grams	Fiber: 1.3 grams
	Total Fat: 2.5 grams	Sodium: 697 mg

Butternut Squash Soup With Ginger & Fennel

Red Pepper & Shiitake Polenta with Roasted Vegetables

Red Pepper & Shiitake Polenta with Roasted Vegetables

Try this lovely dish, packed with color and flavor, for a fall dinner party. Serve with a mixed-greens salad.

PREPARATION TIME: 50–60 MINUTES
SERVES: 6

1 Tbsp	Virgin olive oil
1 medium	Sweet onion, diced
1 cup	Shiitake mushrooms, sliced thinly
1/2 tsp	Sea salt
1/2 tsp	Oregano, dried
1/2 tsp	Rosemary, dried
1 medium	Red bell pepper, chopped
6 cups	Water
2 cups	Polenta (corn meal, coarse)
1/2 cup	Fresh basil and parsley
2 cups	Yellow squash, baby (or small)
2 medium	Carrots, cut into 2-inch pieces
3 medium	Beets, peeled and quartered
1 Tbsp	Virgin olive oil
1/4 tsp	Ground black pepper
1/4 tsp	Sea salt
1/2 tsp	Italian herbs, dried
1 tsp	Virgin olive oil
1 medium	Leek, sliced
1/4 tsp	Sea salt
1/2 tsp	Oregano, dried
2 cups	Green beans, whole
4 medium	Garlic cloves, diced
15 oz	Garbanzo beans, canned, rinsed
1/4 cup	Vegetable stock (see page 139)

Garnish:

1/2 cup	Parsley, chopped
6 Tbsp	Almond slices

Preheat oven to 350°F.

Heat a skillet over medium-high heat and add oil. Sauté onion and mushrooms with salt. Heat 2 minutes. Add herbs and pepper. Stir occasionally. When onion is slightly softened, remove from heat and set aside.

Boil water. Slowly stir in polenta. Reduce heat to low and stir continuously, for 20 minutes. Stir in fresh herbs and mushroom sauté.

Pour cooked polenta on an oil-sprayed cookie sheet, 1/2–1 inch deep, and spread out evenly. Spray the polenta surface for 1–2 seconds with virgin olive oil and smooth the surface with a spatula. Set aside.

Cut squash, carrots, and beets into bite-sized pieces. Place them in a baking dish and combine them with oil, pepper, salt, and dried herbs. Roast uncovered for 20–30 minutes.

Cut polenta into 6 equal squares, cut again into triangles. Spray sauté pan with olive oil, sauté polenta triangles until golden. 10 minutes before serving, place the cookie sheet with polenta triangles in the oven to re-heat. Heat a sauté pan over medium heat and add oil. Sauté the sliced leek, salt, and herbs for 2–3 minutes. Add green beans, garlic, garbanzos, and stock. Heat for 4–5 minutes. Combine with roasted vegetables to keep warm in the oven.

To serve, place 2 polenta triangles on each plate. Mix roasted and sautéed vegetables. Spoon over polenta. Garnish with parsley and almond slices.

Per Serving	Calories: 634	% Fat Calories: 16%
	Saturated Fat: 1.4 grams	Fiber: 21 grams
	Total Fat: 11 grams	Sodium: 647 mg

Mixed Greens Salad with Raspberry Vinaigrette

Choose mixed red and green salad fixings, easy to find already prepared in most grocery stores.

PREPARATION TIME: 5 MINUTES
SERVES: 6

10 cups	**Mixed red and green salad leaves, washed**

Raspberry Vinaigrette:

2 Tbsp	**Balsamic vinegar**
1 Tbsp	**Lemon juice**
1/2 cup	**Raspberries, fresh or frozen**
1 tsp	**Soy sauce, low-sodium**
2 tsp	**Extra virgin olive oil (optional)**
1 clove	**Garlic, minced**
1/2 tsp	**Italian herbs, dried**
1 dash	**Freshly ground black pepper**
1 Tbsp	**Maple syrup**

Place salad leaves in a large bowl.

Mix vinaigrette ingredients in a blender. Toss with salad when ready to serve.

Per Serving

Calories: 54	% Fat Calories: 26%
Saturated Fat: 0.2 grams	Fiber: 2.7 grams
Total Fat: 1.8 grams	Sodium: 51 mg

Pumpkin Pie

Here is a delicious, yet healthy version of pumpkin pie. I like this mostly whole grain crust; if you want your crust lighter, you could use a higher percent of all purpose flour.

PREPARATION TIME: 1 HOUR / BAKING TIME: 65 MINUTES / PIE CHILLING TIME: 2 HOURS
DOUGH REFRIGERATION TIME: 1–24 HOURS
SERVES: 8–10

Crust:

1 cup	Whole wheat pastry flour
3/4 cup	All purpose flour, sifted
1/2 tsp	Sea salt
1/3 cup	Canola oil, chilled
5-6 Tbsp	Water, chilled
1/4 tsp	Sugar
1/8 tsp	Cinnamon

Filling:

15 oz	Pumpkin purée, canned
2/3 cup	Maple syrup
1/2 tsp	Sea salt
1 tsp	Cinnamon
1 Tbsp	Candied ginger root, minced
1/4 tsp	Ground cloves
4 large	Egg whites (or 6 oz firm tofu)
1 cup	Nonfat milk or soy milk

Garnish:

1 cup	Nonfat or non-dairy whipped topping, pressurized

Preheat oven to 400°F.

Crust:
Combine dry crust ingredients. Add chilled oil. Blend with a fork or pastry blender until it has the consistency of cornmeal with pea sized lumps. Handle gently. Don't over mix or the dough becomes tough. Sprinkle dough with water, 1 tablespoon at a time, adding just enough water to be able to form dough into a ball. Wrap in plastic wrap and refrigerate 1–24 hours.

Place dough at room temperature 30–60 minutes before rolling. Between wax paper or plastic wrap, roll dough into a flat circle until it's 2 inches wider than your pie plate. Patch tears but don't re-roll dough. Ease crust into pie plate. Trim border and pinch edges.

Filling:
In a blender, purée filling ingredients then pour into the pie shell. Bake for 15 minutes at 400°F, then lower temperature to 350°F and bake for another 50 minutes. Let cool and solidify at least 2–3 hours in the refrigerator. Serve with a garnish of whipped topping.

Vegan Option:
Substitute 6 ounces of firm tofu for egg whites. Rinse and drain tofu. Crumble it and add to blender with filling ingredients.

Per Serving	Calories: 220	% Fat Calories: 31%
	Saturated Fat: 0.6 grams	Fiber: 2 grams
	Total Fat: 7.7 grams	Sodium: 251 mg

Birthday Dinner Party

I love celebrating my wife's birthday. I can whip up a wonderful meal, invite friends over, and celebrate how special she is. This Mushroom-Pecan Paté, wrapped delicately with leeks in fillo dough provides the perfect dinner packet for a birthday party. A birthday cake with candles is a must! This chocolate cake with brandied cherries and hazelnuts is a grand way to enjoy any birthday celebration. The meal as a whole is flavorful, surprisingly low-fat, and tantalizing.

Birthday Dinner Party Menu

Bell Pepper & Artichoke Spread on Pita Bread

✤

Mushroom-Pecan Paté Wrapped in Fillo

✤

Broccoli with Wild Mushrooms, Herbs & Almond Slices

✤

Mashed Potatoes with Garlic & Herbs

✤

Chocolate Cake with Mocha Icing

Birthday Dinner Party Preparation Plan

Plan on 4–5 hours of preparation time. Consider asking your guests to bring dancing shoes. Play music between hors d'oeuvres and dinner, or between dinner and dessert. For a shopping list, see page 148.

1–2 DAYS BEFORE THE PARTY (1 1/2–2 HOURS PREP TIME)
- Make gravy.
- Make paté.
- Sauté leeks and mushrooms for fillo wrapping.
- Make cherry filling for cake.
- Seal and refrigerate items in separate containers.

MORNING OF PARTY (1 HOUR PREP TIME)
- Bake cake. Make cake frosting and assemble cake. I prefer to bake the cake layers the day of the party. You can bake them the day before, and wrap and store in the refrigerator or freezer.

2 HOURS BEFORE THE PARTY
- Prepare red pepper and artichoke spread.
- Slice mushrooms and broccoli for side dish and set aside.
- Cut potatoes into 1-inch cubes and cover with water in a large pot. Bring to a boil, cooking potatoes until soft.
- Assemble pecan paté wrapped in fillo. Place on a cookie sheet. Cover with plastic wrap.
- Sauté garlic and herbs for mashed potatoes and set aside.

30 MINUTES BEFORE THE PARTY
- Open red wine, and/or place sparkling cider or champagne in the refrigerator.
- Preheat oven to 375°F for fillo wrapped paté.
- Lightly toast pita bread and serve with spreads. Chop parsley for garnishes.

20 MINUTES BEFORE SERVING DINNER
- Reheat potatoes.
- Place the fillo wrapped paté in the oven.
- Simmer gravy on low heat, add extra stock if overly thick.

10 MINUTES BEFORE SERVING DINNER
- Begin sautéing mushrooms and broccoli.
- Whip reheated potatoes, whipping in garlic and herbs.
- Warm plates in the oven (optional).

TO SERVE
- Pipe or spoon mashed potatoes on one-third of the plate. Add mushroom and broccoli sauté to another third. Add fillo-paté to the final third.
- Drizzle gravy over the fillo wrapped paté and potatoes.
- Sprinkle almond slices over fillo-paté and mushroom/broccoli sauté.
- Sprinkle chopped parsley over plates.
- Fill a serving bowl with remaining gravy.

Bell Pepper & Artichoke Spread on Pita Bread

Easy to prepare, and tasty. This is also a wonderful spread in sandwiches.

PREPARATION TIME: 15 MINUTES
SERVES: APPETIZER FOR 8

Spread:

3 large	Red bell peppers, roasted
15 oz	Artichoke hearts, cooked
1/4 cup	Parmesan cheese, grated (optional)
3 medium	Garlic cloves, minced
1 Tbsp	Extra virgin olive oil
1 Tbsp	Lemon juice, fresh
1/4 tsp	Sea salt
1/2 cup	Parsley, fresh

Garnish:

2 Tbsp	Capers
Few sprigs	Parsley
2-3 rounds	Whole wheat pita bread

Combine spread ingredients in a food processor or blender and process until smooth, to the consistency of a spread. For directions on roasting peppers, see page 138. If you don't use the parmesan cheese, you could add 1 additional tablespoon of extra virgin olive oil.

Transfer to a serving bowl, garnish with capers and sprigs of parsley. Serve with triangle-cut wedges of pita bread.

Per Serving

Calories: 138		% Fat Calories: 20%
Saturated Fat: 0.8 grams		Sodium: 252 mg
Total Fat: 3.4 gram		Fiber: 5.6 grams

Birthday Dinner

Mushroom-Pecan Paté Wrapped in Fillo

This is a lovely package for a birthday dinner. This paté stores well in the refrigerator for up to a week. I adapted this recipe from the menu at Seattle's Café Flora, after having worked in their wonderful restaurant for a month. I have included a vegan variation at the end of the recipe.

PREPARATION TIME: 1 HOUR / PATÉ CHILLING TIME: 1-3 HOURS
BAKING TIME: 1 HOUR
SERVES: 8

Paté:

1 Tbsp	Virgin olive oil
1 medium	Onion, diced
4 cups	Mushrooms, minced
2 medium	Carrots, minced
4 medium	Garlic cloves, minced
1/2 tsp	Sea salt
1/4 tsp	Ground pepper
1 tsp	Italian herbs, dried
1/2 cup	Port wine
8 large	Egg whites, beaten lightly
1/2 cup	Nonfat mozzarella cheese, grated (or soy cheese)
3 oz	Pecans, roasted and chopped
1 cup	Whole wheat bread crumbs

Sauté:

1 tsp	Virgin olive oil
2 cups	Leeks, sliced (white part only)
2 cups	Shiitake (or Chanterelle) mushrooms, sliced thinly
1/4 tsp	Sea salt
12 sheets	Fillo dough

Garnish:

	Vegetarian gravy (see page 11)
1/2 cup	Parsley, chopped
4 Tbsp	Cranberries, dried

Preheat oven to 375°F.

Heat a sauté pan over medium-high heat and add oil. Sauté onion, mushrooms, and carrots for 3–4 minutes until onion turns soft and golden. Reduce heat to medium. Add garlic, salt, pepper, herbs and sauté 2 more minutes. Add port to sauté, reduce (thicken) 5–10 minutes. Set aside.

Combine egg whites with grated cheese, roasted pecans, and bread crumbs. Add to sauté, mixing well.

Line a loaf pan with parchment or wax paper. Spray paper for 2 seconds with virgin olive oil. Pour in paté mixture. Bake for 40 minutes, until a toothpick comes out clean. Let cool several hours in the refrigerator to solidify.

Heat a sauté pan over medium-high heat and add oil. Sauté leeks, mushrooms and salt until soft, about 4 minutes. Set aside. After paté has solidified, cut into 8 slices, 1-inch thick.

Place fillo on a dry surface. Make 2 stacks containing 6 sheets of fillo each. Spray each sheet (1–2 seconds) with olive oil spray. With a sharp knife, cut each stack into 4 equal pieces (you should have 8 stacks, approximately 6x8 inches each).

Add 1 slice of paté on top of each stack and cover paté with 2 tablespoons of sautéed leeks and mushrooms. Wrap paté in fillo loosely, forming a fillo-wrapped package. Place packages on a cookie sheet with the loose edges of the fillo facing up. Spray the top of each package with virgin olive oil spray. Bake for about 20 minutes, until packages are golden brown. Serve with gravy and garnish with parsley and cranberries.

Vegan Option:

Prepare sauté as outlined. Instead of pre-baking the paté, substitute 6 ounces of firm tofu for the egg whites. Rinse and drain tofu then pat it dry with paper towels to remove excess moisture. Purée the tofu then combine it with soy cheese, pecans and bread crumbs. Mix this tofu mixture with the rest of the sauté ingredients. (Do not bake this mixture.)

Prepare the fillo sheets as outlined above. Spoon 8 divided portions of the sauté-tofu mixture onto the 8 prepared fillo sheets. Add the 2 tablespoons of leek-mushroom sauté mixture on top. Wrap mixture with fillo sheets as described above and bake until golden. Garnish as described.

Per Serving	Calories: 342	% Fat Calories: 33%
	Saturated Fat: 1.4 grams	Fiber: 3.8 grams
	Total Fat: 12.6 grams	Sodium: 565 mg

Mixed Packages, Mushroom-Pecan Paté Wrapped in Fillo

Broccoli with Wild Mushrooms, Herbs & Almond Slices

Start 8–10 minutes before you serve the fillo wrapped paté. Use any variety of wild mushrooms.

PREPARATION TIME: 5 MINUTES
COOKING TIME: 7 MINUTES
SERVES: 8

1/2 tsp	**Virgin olive oil**
1 cup	**Wild mushrooms, sliced**
1/2 tsp	**Dill weed**
1/4 tsp	**Sea salt**
4 cups	**Broccoli, sliced into long strips**
1 Tbsp	**Almond slices, roasted**

Heat a sauté pan over medium-high heat and add oil. Sauté mushrooms, herbs and salt for 2 minutes. Add broccoli and cook for 3–5 minutes, until al dente. Place in a serving bowl or on individual plates. Garnish with almond slices.

Per Serving   Calories: 26   % Fat Calories: 16%
Saturated Fat: 0   Fiber: 4.4 grams
Total Fat: 0.6 grams   Sodium: 36 mg

Mashed Potatoes with Garlic & Herbs

These mashed potatoes are light and flavorful. Use the vegetarian gravy recipe listed on page 11.

PREPARATION TIME: 20–30 MINUTES
SERVES: 8

4 medium	**Russet potatoes, peeled**
6 medium	**Garlic cloves, diced**
1 tsp	**Thyme**
1 Tbsp	**Virgin olive oil**
1 cup	**Nonfat milk (or soy milk)**
1/2 tsp	**Sea salt**
1/8 tsp	**Ground pepper**
1/2 cup	**Fresh basil, chopped finely**
Garnish:	
2 Tbsp	**Cranberries, dried**

Peel and cube potatoes, cover with water in a pot, bring to a boil, and simmer until soft. Mash or whip.

Sauté garlic and thyme in oil over medium heat for 1 minute, until garlic is yellow but not browned.

While whipping potatoes, whip in sautéed garlic, then whip in milk, salt, pepper, and fresh herbs. Pipe on individual plates, or serve in a bowl. Serve with vegetarian gravy.

Per Serving   Calories: 185   % Fat Calories: 20%
Saturated Fat: 0   Fiber: 3.6 gram
Total Fat: 3.8 grams   Sodium: 927 mg

Chocolate Cake with Mocha Icing

Chocolate Cake with Mocha Icing

This is our favorite vegan cake recipe. Nicole and I have worked on it over the years. It is moist, delicious, and easy to make. This cake is surprisingly rich, while featuring only thirty-one percent of its calories from healthy fat.

PREPARATION TIME: 1 HOUR
BAKING TIME: 25–30 MINUTES
SERVES: 12

Cake:

1 cup	Whole wheat pastry flour
1 cup	All purpose flour
1 cup	Sugar
1 tsp	Sea salt
2 tsp	Baking powder
2 1/2 tsp	Baking soda
1/2 cup	Cocoa powder
1/3 cup	Canola oil
1 cup	White wine
1 1/2 cups	Soy milk (Or, nonfat milk)
1 Tbsp	Vanilla extract

Filling:

2 cups	Cherries (fresh or frozen), finely chopped
1/4 cup	Sugar
4 Tbsp	Rum, dark
1 tsp	Vanilla extract

Frosting:

8 oz	Semi-sweet chocolate
1/4 cup	Strong coffee or espresso, brewed
1/3 cup	Sugar

Garnish:

1/4 oz	Chocolate shavings
1/2 cup	Fresh cherries, or berries
3 Tbsp	Hazelnuts, coarsely chopped

Preheat oven to 375°F.

Cake:
Combine dry cake ingredients and sift them through a fine mesh strainer (in order not to lose the flour bran). In a separate bowl, whisk liquid ingredients until foamy. Combine with dry ingredients by slowly pouring into the bowl and stirring until batter is well mixed. Pour batter into two 9-inch cake pans sprayed with canola oil and dusted with flour. Bake 25–30 minutes, until toothpick comes out clean. Cool on cake racks for 5 minutes. Remove from pans and allow to cool completely.

Filling:
Place cherries and sugar in a saucepan and cook over medium-low heat until mixture has reduced to a thick syrup, about 30 minutes. Remove from heat and stir in rum and vanilla. Set aside.

Frosting:
Melt chocolate in a double boiler. Remove from heat as soon as chocolate has melted. In a separate pan, warm sugar and coffee until all sugar has dissolved. Pour liquid into melted chocolate and stir until well mixed. Set aside.

Assembly:
Roast chopped nuts in the oven for 5–6 minutes, or the microwave for 1 minute. When cakes have cooled, set first cake layer on a platter. Spread filling over top. Place second cake layer on first layer. Spread frosting on the cake. Place cooled, roasted nuts evenly around sides of cake. With a vegetable peeler, shave 1/4 ounce of chocolate over cake and garnish with cherries. Chill the cake in the refrigerator. Serve with candles!

Per Serving	Calories: 418	% Fat Calories: 31%
	Saturated Fat: 4 grams	Fiber: 5 grams
	Total Fat: 14 grams	Sodium: 510 mg

Holiday Party Hors D'Oeuvres

During the month of December, there seem to be endless holiday parties. Here are a few of my favorite hors d'oeuvres recipes for these special gatherings. Enjoy them anytime of year.

Holiday Party Hors D'Oeuvres

Cherry Tomatoes Stuffed with Potato, Cheese & Herbs

❖

Stuffed Grape Leaves with Eggplant Dip

❖

Avocado Dip with Jicama

❖

Roasted Pepper Terrine (see page 5)

❖

Sushi Rice Rolls (see page 49)

Cherry Tomatoes Stuffed with Potato, Cheese & Herbs

This is a cheerful and tasty dish for a holiday party.

PREPARATION TIME: 30 MINUTES
MAKES: 20 BITE-SIZED APPETIZERS

1 small	Russet potato
1 tsp	Virgin olive oil
1/2 small	White onion, minced
1/2 tsp	Sea salt
1 tsp	Italian herbs, dried
4 Tbsp	Italian parsley, finely chopped
20 medium	Cherry tomatoes
2 Tbsp	Parmesan cheese, finely grated (or soy cheese)
1 bunch	Chives, cut into 1-inch pieces

Peel and cube potato. Boil until very soft. Mash, or whip in a food processor.

Meanwhile, heat a skillet over medium heat and add oil. Add onion and salt. Sauté 3–4 minutes, until onion turns yellow. Add herbs and heat 1 minute. Set aside.

Slice a sliver off the bottom of each cherry tomato to form a flat base. Slice off the top third of the tomato. Set base and top aside. Repeat this process with each tomato.

Combine potato, sautéed onion, and grated cheese. Spoon or pipe 1/2 teaspoon filling over each tomato base and cover with top hat. Garnish with herbs.

Arrange on a serving plate. Garnish plate with remaining chives and a few sprigs of parsley.

Per Serving
(3 tomatoes)

Calories: 141
Saturated Fat: 0.6 grams
Total Fat: 2.9 grams

% Fat Calories: 16%
Fiber: 6.3 grams
Sodium: 275 mg

Cherry Tomatoes Stuffed with Potato, Cheese & Herbs

Stuffed Grape Leaves with Eggplant Dip

This appetizer compliments any party. Vary the ingredients inside the grape leaves as you like. The eggplant dip provides twice what you need, so you can also use it as a dip for raw vegetables such as carrots and broccoli.

PREPARATION TIME: 1 HOUR
BAKING TIME: 1 HOUR
SERVES: APPETIZER FOR 6

1/2 cup	**Brown rice**
1/2 cup	**Bulgur wheat**

Eggplant dip:

1 medium	**Eggplant**
8 oz	**Garbanzo beans, cooked or canned, drained**
1/2 tsp	**Sea salt**
1/4 tsp	**Freshly ground black pepper**
1/4 tsp	**Ground cumin**
1 medium	**Garlic clove, minced**
2 medium	**Lemons, juiced**
2 Tbsp	**Extra virgin olive oil**
2 Tbsp	**Sesame tahini**

Stuffed grape leaves:

1 tsp	**Virgin olive oil**
1 medium	**Onion, finely diced**
1/2 tsp	**Sea salt**
1 tsp	**Italian herbs, dried**
4 medium	**Garlic cloves, minced**
1/2 cup	**Italian parsley, chopped**
1/4 cup	**Walnuts, chopped**
24 medium	**Grape leaves (8 oz from a jar with brine. Rinse brine from leaves and drain)**

Garnish:	**Dashes of paprika**

Preheat oven to 375°F.

In a saucepan, bring water and brown rice to a boil. Reduce heat and simmer covered for 40 minutes. Set aside.
In a separate saucepan, bring 1/2 cup water to a boil. Add bulgur, reduce heat, and simmer 5 minutes. Remove from heat and set aside covered for 15 minutes.

Eggplant dip:
Slice eggplant in half, prick pulp with a fork, and bake 35 minutes. After baking, scoop pulp into a blender, discarding skin. Purée with garbanzo beans, salt, pepper, cumin, garlic, lemon juice, oil, and sesame tahini. Spoon into a serving bowl and refrigerate.

Stuffed grape leaves:
Heat a skillet over medium heat and add oil. Add onion, salt, and Italian herbs. Sauté for 3–4 minutes. Add garlic, parsley, and walnuts. Heat 1 minute. Combine with cooked rice and bulgur. Set aside.

On a flat surface, place a grape leaf in front of you with the stem pointing toward you. Add 1–2 tablespoons of mixture to the center of each grape leaf. Fold the right bottom edge toward the left-center, then fold the left bottom edge toward the right-center, making a 2-inch long triangle. Roll the stem side of the leaf away from you towards the leaf tip, forming a bundle.

Set stuffed grape leaves in a baking dish and bake at 250°F for 1 hour. Serve hot or cold. Serve with eggplant dip garnished with a dash of paprika.

Per Serving	Calories: 318	% Fat Calories: 33%
	Saturated Fat: 1.3 grams	Fiber: 11 grams
	Total Fat: 11.5 grams	Sodium: 275 mg

Avocado Dip with Jicama

If preparing in advance, add the avocado just before serving as cut avocado doesn't store well. Serve with your favorite raw vegetables and jicama slices.

PREPARATION TIME: 10 MINUTES
SERVES: 8

1 large	**Lime, juiced**
1/2 tsp	**Sea salt**
1/8 tsp	**Chili powder**
1/3 cup	**Nonfat yogurt (optional)**
2 medium	**Tomatoes, chopped**
1/2 medium	**Onion, finely diced**
1/4 cup	**Fresh cilantro, chopped**
2 medium	**Ripe avocados**
1–2 cups	**Baby carrots**
1 large	**Red bell pepper, sliced into thin strips**
1 medium	**Jicama, sliced into dip sized pieces**

Garnish:

1/8 tsp	**Chili powder**
1 tsp	**Fresh cilantro**

In a bowl, combine lime juice, salt, chile, yogurt, tomato, onion, and cilantro and mix together. Just before serving, slice avocados in half, discard seed, then scoop out avocado. Mash in a bowl and combine with above ingredients.

Spoon avocado dip into a bowl in the center of a large platter. Arrange carrots, pepper, and jicama around the platter.

Garnish dip with a dash of paprika or chile powder and fresh cilantro sprigs.

Per Serving	Calories: 264	% Fat Calories: 31%
	Saturated Fat: 1.5 grams	Fiber: 8 grams
	Total Fat: 9.8 grams	Sodium: 288 mg

Holiday Food Gifts

Make time to prepare food gifts for friends over the holiday season. With planning, you can make some of these special treats in the summer when fruit is at its peak and store for later. Here are a few of our favorite recipes.

Holiday Food Gifts

Kumquat-Ginger Marmalade

✛

Mango Chutney

✛

Blackberry & Blueberry Jam

✛

Dried Fruit-Nut Balls

✛

Chocolate with Candied Ginger & Dried Cherries

Kumquat-Ginger Marmalade

This is a great marmalade any time of year. Look for organic kumquats in early December to make a special holiday gift.

PREPARATION TIME: 1 HOUR
SIMMERING TIME: 30 MINUTES
MAKES: 8–9 CUPS

4 cups	Kumquats
2 1/2 cups	Water
1/2 cup	Candied ginger root
1/8 tsp	Baking soda
1 Tbsp	Almond oil
1 package	Sure-Jell® Fruit Pectin (Low-sugar pectins use less sugar. The type of pectin determines your sugar/pectin ratio–follow the directions.)
4 cups	Sugar
1/4 cup	Grand Marnier
9 1-cup	Canning jars with lids

Sterilize jars, lids, ladle, and wide-mouthed funnel. Keep jars in boiling water until ready to use. (See cooking supplies page 133.)

Quarter kumquats lengthwise. Remove seeds. Bring kumquats and water to a boil in a large pot and simmer 20 minutes. Skim off any remaining seeds.

Finely chop candied ginger (easiest in a food processor). Coarsely chop kumquats, leaving small pieces.

Return ginger and kumquats to simmering pot. Stir in baking soda, oil, and pectin. Bring to a brisk boil. Add sugar and Grand Marnier, bring to a boil again, then simmer 10 minutes.

Fill jars with ladle within 1/4-inch of top. Place lids and tighten firmly. Let cool 24 hours. Check lids by pressing down on the center of the lid. If it springs up, it did not seal and should be refrigerated and eaten soon.

Mango Chutney

This is a lovely condiment for curry dishes. Best to make in the summer when mangos are ripe and inexpensive.

PREPARATION AND CANNING TIME: 1 1/2 hours
YIELDS: 12 CUPS

1 1/3 cups	Sugar
1 cup	Cider Vinegar
2 medium	Limes, juiced
1 tsp	Ground Cloves
1 tsp	Ground cardamom
1 tsp	Cardamom seeds
1 tsp	Cayenne pepper
1 tsp	Sea salt
8 large	Mangos, firm, not over ripe
4 Tbsp	Ginger root, peeled and minced
2 cups	Onion, minced
1 cup	Raisins
1 cup	Dried Cranberries

Mango and Ginger

Have ready a large canning pot with water and bring to a boil. Sterilize the utensils you will use including canning jars and lids. (See cooking supplies page 133.) You can use any size canning jars you like, yielding 12 cups.

In a large saucepan, bring the sugar, vinegar, lime juice, cloves, cardamom, cayenne, and salt to a boil, then lower heat and simmer for 30 minutes.

Meanwhile, peel mangos and remove pulp from the seed. Dice pulp and combine with the minced ginger, onion, raisins, and cranberries. Add these to the vinegar solution and bring to a boil once more. Lower heat and simmer for another 5 minutes.

As soon as the chutney is done simmering, remove the sterilized jars and set them on the counter. Carefully fill each jar with the chutney allowing only about 1/4 to 1/2 inch of space from the rim. To ensure rims are perfectly clean, wipe them with a wet paper towel (dipped in the boiling water), then immediately seal the jars with the new, sterilized canning lids, and hand tighten.

Place the filled jars in a boiling water bath for 5 minutes (be sure the water is at a rolling boil and that you have each jar covered with at least 2 inches of water from the top of the jar to the surface).

Remove jars from the water and allow to cool. Once the jars have cooled, check each lid to make sure it sealed properly. The jars should have created a vacuum and the lids should be flat. You are now ready to label and date your jars.

Blackberry & Blueberry Jam

Blueberry and blackberry make a wonderful combination. What's more, they are great for your health. Enjoy this jam often.

PREPARATION TIME: 45 MINUTES
YIELDS: 7–8 CUPS

2 1/2 cups	**Blackberries, fresh or frozen**
3 1/2 cups	**Blueberries, fresh or frozen**
1/4 cup	**Sugar**
1 package	**Sure-Jell® Fruit Pectin (Low-sugar pectins use less sugar. The type of pectin determines your sugar/ pectin ratio–follow the directions.)**
3 Tbsp	**Lemon juice**
1 Tbsp	**Lemon rind, grated**
2 tsp	**Almond oil (or canola oil)**
4 cups	**Sugar**
2-3 Tbsp	**Candied ginger, finely minced**

Cooking Supplies:

8 1-cup	**Jars with lids**
1 large	**Mixing bowl**
1 medium	**Ladle**
1 large	**Wide-mouthed funnel, jar sized**
1	**Masher or food processor**
1 medium	**Pot**
1 medium	**Spatula**

Sterilize jars in boiling water. Add ladle, lids and wide-mouthed funnel to near boiling water. Keep jars and lids in boiling water until ready to use.

If you use frozen berries, thaw well. Purée half the blackberries in a food processor, or mash by hand. Then, stirring with a spatula, mash puréed blackberries through a sieve to remove seeds.

In a large sauce pan, combine 1/4 cup of sugar with 1 box of Sure-Jell® pectin. Stir in remaining blackberries, blueberries, lemon juice and lemon rind, oil, and candied ginger. Bring to a rolling boil, stirring constantly.

Add remaining sugar, bring to a rolling boil. Stir for 1 minute.

Immediately remove sauce pan from heat, skim off any foam, and with a ladle and a wide-mouthed funnel, start filling jars within 1/4-inch of top. Tighten lids firmly and turn jars upside down for 5 minutes. Then turn right-side-up. Let cool 24 hours.

Check lids by pressing down on the center of the lid. If it springs up, it did not seal and should be refrigerated and eaten soon.

Dried Fruit-Nut Balls

These fruit-nut balls are fun to make and my boys enjoy helping. Vary the dried fruit and nuts as you like.

PREPARATION TIME: 20 MINUTES
MAKES: 65 BALLS

1/2 cup	**Almond flour**
1/2 cup	**Dried cherries**
1/2 cup	**Dried figs**
2 Tbsp	**Powdered sugar**
2 tsp	**Lemon juice**
1 Tbsp	**Rum (or 1 tsp orange extract)**
2 oz	**Semi-sweet chocolate**
1/4 cup	**Hazelnuts, finely chopped**

In a food processor, process 3/5 cup of almonds to make 1/2 cup of almond flour, or buy prepared almond flour. Add dried cherries and figs and process again. Stir in sugar, lemon juice, and rum.

Melt chocolate and blend with purée. Roll mixture into hazelnut sized balls, 1 1/2 tsp per ball. (Messy but fun!)

On a cookie sheet, spread out chopped hazelnuts. Roll fruit-nut balls in chopped hazelnuts, forming a delicate nut covering.

Freeze or refrigerate fruit-nut balls until ready to serve.

Per Serving	Calories: 100	% Fat Calories: 20%
(2 nut balls)	Saturated Fat: 0.8 mg.	Fiber: 1.2 grams
	Total Fat: 2.4 grams	Sodium: 0

Lucas Making Dried Fruit-Nut Balls

Chocolate with Candied Ginger & Dried Cherries

Here is one of my favorite special treats! Easy to make and fabulous. Splurge on the best chocolate and candied ginger you can find.

<small>Preparation Time: 10–15 minutes</small>
<small>Makes: 24 Treats</small>

10 oz	**Semi-sweet chocolate**
1/2 cup	**Candied ginger, chopped into various sized bits**
1/2 cup	**Dried cherries and/or blueberries**

Heat chocolate in a double boiler (or very slowly in a pan) until creamy.

Cover 2 cookie trays with parchment paper. Spoon 1 teaspoon of candied ginger and 1 teaspoon of dried berries into mounds. Drizzle 1 Tbsp of chocolate over each mound. Garnish top with a sliver of ginger and a dried cherry.

Place trays in the freezer for 20 minutes to harden chocolates. Store in the refrigerator. Serve these treats chilled or they melt on your fingertips.

Per Serving (2/serving)	Calories: 147	% Fat Calories: 46%
	Saturated Fat: 2.2 grams	Fiber: 2 grams
	Total Fat: 7.2 grams	Sodium: 0

Chocolate with Candied Ginger & Dried Cherries

"Petite Mama Picking Fruit," by Annouchka Galouchko

Appendices & Shopping Lists

Roasting Peppers

Roasted peppers go very well with Mexican and Mediterranean dishes. They are sweet, delicious, and loaded with antioxidants.

Set oven on broil.

If you are going to use the roasted peppers for stuffing:
Place whole peppers in a rimmed broiler-proof pan (to catch the pepper juice.) Place the pan on the top rack of the oven. Roast until skin browns, then turn. Repeat process until all the sides are browned (about 12 minutes.) Remove from the oven. Set aside and allow to cool. Remove skin and discard. With a sharp knife, cut a slit along the pepper and gently scoop out the seeds. Discard seeds. Leave the stem attached.

If you are not going to stuff the peppers:
Cut off pepper crown with the stem, and scoop out seeds. Place peppers in a rimmed broiler-proof pan (to catch the pepper juice.) Place on the top rack of the oven. Roast until skin browns, then turn. Repeat process until all the sides are browned (about 12 minutes.) Remove from the oven. Set aside and allow to cool. Remove skin and discard.

You can roast a dozen peppers at a time and refrigerate or freeze what you don't use in individual packets for later use. You can chop peppers for stir fry, bake them in corn bread, or purée them for dip.

Peppers

Vegetable Stock

Vegetable stock is needed in many recipes. You can use ready made powdered varieties, broth cubes, or make your own delicious version. If you use pre-made stock, look for low-sodium brands. Whenever you steam vegetables, save the residue water as liquid for future stock. Don't hesitate to vary the vegetable ingredients listed below. Try adding fennel, or other root vegetables to create your own favorite flavors. For a clear stock, omit the tomato sauce.

PREPARATION TIME: 15 MINUTES
SIMMERING TIME: 1 HOUR
MAKES: 6 CUPS

1 medium	Onion, diced
4 medium	Garlic cloves, diced
3 medium	Leek green tops, chopped
1 medium	Potato, cubed
2 medium	Carrots, diced
1/2 cup	Tomato sauce
1 cup	Mushrooms, finely chopped
2 tsp	Virgin olive oil
1 tsp	Italian herbs, dried (thyme, basil, rosemary, oregano)
6 cups	Warm water
1–3 Tbsp	Miso*

Peel and dice the onion and garlic. Chop leek greens, potato, carrots, tomato, and mushrooms.

Heat a soup pot, and add oil. Sauté cut vegetables over medium heat. Stir in the herbs and heat for 2–3 minutes, then cover and simmer for 10 minutes. Add the water and bring to a boil. Reduce heat to a simmer. Stir in the miso* paste and simmer for 1 hour. For a delicately flavored soup, like garlic soup, only add 1/2–1 tablespoon of miso paste. For a hearty soup that will have rice or noodles, add 2–3 tablespoons of miso. After simmering, strain the stock. Discard vegetables.

Use the stock immediately, or store in the refrigerator or freezer in a sealed container.

Do not use miso for Passover dishes—instead, substitute 1/2 teaspoon of salt for 1 tablespoon miso.

Per Serving	Calories: 58	% Fat Calories: 20%
	Saturated Fat: 0	Fiber: 0
	Total Fat: 1.3 grams	Sodium: 356 mg

Shopping Lists

Thanksgiving Shopping List

delete items if preparing vegan option

brown sugar	2/3 cup
sugar	1 cup
flour, all purpose	3/4 cup
flour, whole wheat pastry	1 2/3 cups
port wine	3 Tbsp
red wine	1 1/2 cups
bread crumbs, whole wheat	2 cups
black beans, canned	15 oz
stewed tomatoes, canned	15 oz
canola oil	1/2 cup
olive oil spray	1 can
olive oil, virgin	4 Tbsp
*egg whites	7 large
*nonfat milk	1 1/2 cups
wild rice	1/2 cup
dried cranberries	1/3 cup
dried cherries	2/3 cup
fillo dough (frozen pastries)	12 sheets
blueberries, frozen	1 cup
cherries, frozen	4 cups
cranberries, frozen	16 oz
quinoa (grains)	1/2 cup
almonds	1/2 cup
almonds, sliced	2 Tbsp
cashews	1/2 cup
pecans	1 cup
walnuts	1/4 cup
soy sauce, low sodium	4 Tbsp
apples, granny smith	6 cups
basil, fresh	1/2 cup
bell peppers, orange, for roasting	4 large
broccoli flowerets	2 cups
butternut squash	3 medium
carrots	3 medium
cilantro, fresh	4 1/2 cups
garlic	2 heads
ginger root, fresh	1 Tbsp
leeks	2 medium
lemon juice	1 Tbsp
lime	1 small
mint, fresh	1/2 cup
miso paste (produce)	2 Tbsp
mushrooms	4 cups
mushrooms, shiitake	3 cups
onions	2 medium
oranges	2 medium
orange juice	3 cups
parsley, fresh	3/4 cup
potatoes, russet	6 medium
tofu, firm	10 oz
tomatoes	2 medium
vegetable stock	2 3/4 cups
chili powder	1 Tbsp
cinnamon	1/8 tsp
cumin powder	1 tsp
cumin seed	1 tsp
ground pepper	1/4 tsp
Italian herbs	4 tsp
nutmeg	1/8 tsp
sea salt	3 1/2 tsp
cornstarch	2 tsp
rice vinegar	4 Tbsp

vegan option:

soy milk	1 1/2 cups
tofu, firm	6 oz

Christmas Eve Shopping List

delete items if preparing vegan option

baking powder	1 tsp
baking soda	1/2 tsp
chocolate, semi-sweet	2 oz
flour, all purpose	1/2 cup
flour, whole wheat pastry	1 cup
vanilla extract	1/2 tsp
bread loaf, whole grain	1 large
bread crumbs, whole wheat	1/2 cup
apple cider or juice	6 cups

olive oil spray	1 can
olive oil, virgin	1/4 cup
canola oil	1/3 cup
*milk, nonfat	1 1/2 cups
*cheese, nonfat, mozzarella	1/2 cup
* cheese, Parmesan	5 Tbsp
*egg whites	10 large
*wild rice	1 cup
prunes	6 medium
*quinoa (grains)	1 cup
rum, dark	1/3 cup
almonds, sliced	3 Tbsp
hazelnuts	1/4 cup
apricots, frozen	1 cup
cranberries, frozen	6 oz
bell pepper, red	1 medium
berries, fresh	1/4 cup
fennel bulb	1 medium
garlic	3 heads
*garlic cloves	5 medium
ginger, fresh	1 Tbsp
kale (purple or green)	3 cups
leeks	2 medium
mint, fresh	1 Tbsp
*miso paste (produce)	1/2 Tbsp
mushrooms, shiitake	3 cups
*onion, red	1 medium
oranges	2 medium
orange juice	1 cup
*parsley, fresh	1 cup
parsley, fresh	1 1/2 cups
pears, Bartlett, ripe	6 small
scallions	7 medium
vegetable stock	7 cups
cinnamon stick	1 medium
cloves, whole	1/2 teaspoon
dill weed	1 teaspoon
ginger, candied	1 Tbsp
Italian herbs	2 teaspoons
saffron	2 pinches
salt	1 1/4 tsp
maple syrup	2/3 cup

vegan Option:

wine, white	1/4 cup
olive oil, virgin	2 Tbsp
soy milk	1 1/2 cups

rice, arborio	2 cups
pecans	1/4 cup
herbs, fresh (parsley, basil)	1/4 cup
onion	1 medium
spinach, fresh	8 cups
squash, butternut	1 large
squash, baby yellow	2 cups
black pepper, ground	1/8 tsp
Italian herbs, dried	1 tsp
sea salt	1/4 tsp
vegetable stock	6 cups

Christmas Morning Shopping List
*delete items if preparing vegan option

olive oil, extra virgin	2 tsp
*yogurt, nonfat, lemon	1 cup
*yogurt, nonfat, plain	1 1/4 cup
bagels, whole wheat	8 medium
cinnamon toast	1 package
mandarin orange slices, canned	14 oz
apples	2 medium
bell peppers, red, for roasting	2 medium
leeks	3 medium
lime	1 medium
mint, fresh	1/2 cup
pear, Asian	1 medium
pear, Bartlett or Bosc	1 medium
pomegranate	1 small
orange juice, fresh squeezed	2 quarts
kumquat (or orange) marmalade	1 jar
Italian herbs, dried	1/4 tsp
sea salt	1/8 tsp

Christmas Breakfast Shopping list
*delete items if preparing vegan option

rum or brandy, dark	2/3 cup
sparkling cider	1 bottle

canola oil	1 Tbsp
virgin olive oil	3 Tbsp
*egg substitute (or 14 egg whites)	2 cups
soy sausage	1–2 packages
bell pepper, red	1 large
fennel bulb and stalk	3 cups
garlic cloves	4 medium
mushrooms, shiitake	2 cups
onion	1 medium
orange	1 medium
orange juice	1 qt
potatoes, red	18 small
prunes, pitted	6 oz
cherries, dried	1 cup
raisins	1 cup
pecans	1/2 cup
almonds	1/2 cup
allspice, ground	1/4 tsp
cinnamon, ground	1/4 tsp
ginger powder	1/4 tsp
Italian herbs, dried	1/2 tsp
nutmeg, ground	1/4 tsp
pepper, ground	1 tsp
rosemary, fresh or dry	1 Tbsp
sea salt	1 tsp
turmeric	1 tsp

vegan option:

tofu, firm	1 lb

Christmas Dinner Shopping List
delete items if preparing vegan option

baking powder	1 tsp
baking soda	1 1/2 tsp
chocolate, semi-sweet	4 oz
cocoa powder, unsweetened	1/4 cup
flour, all purpose	1/2 cup
flour, whole wheat pastry	1 1/2 cups
sugar	3/4 cup
vanilla extract	2 1/2 tsp
wine, white	3/4 cup

canola oil	5 Tbsp
olive oil, extra virgin	1 Tbsp
olive oil, virgin	4 Tbsp
*cheese mozzarella, nonfat	1/2 cup
*cheese, parmesan	3/4 cup
*egg whites	3 large
*milk, nonfat	3 1/3 cups
whipped topping, pressurized, nonfat	1 can
cranberries, frozen	6 oz
rum, dark	3 Tbsp
almonds, sliced	5 Tbsp
bell pepper, red	1 medium
beets	4 medium
carrots	3 medium
chestnuts, fresh or canned	10 oz
garlic cloves	3 medium
ginger, fresh	1 Tbsp
green beans	4 cups
kale, purple	1 cup
leeks	2 medium
lemon	1 small
mint, fresh	1 Tbsp
mushrooms, shiitake	1 cup
onions	3 medium
orange	1 medium
orange juice	1/2 cup
parsley, fresh	1/2 cup
potatoes, russet	5 medium
scallions	6 medium
yams	5 medium
vegetable stock	6 3/4 cups
dill weed	1/2 tsp
ginger powder	1 tsp
Italian herbs, dried	2 1/2 tsp
sea salt	3 tsp
maple syrup	1/4 cup

vegan option:

soy milk	3 cups
soy mozzarella	1/2 cup
soy parmesan cheese	1/2 cup
flax seeds	2 Tbsp

New Year's Eve Party Shopping List

delete items if preparing vegan option

*cocoa powder, dutch processed	1/2 cup
*flour, all purpose	2 Tbsp
*sugar	1 cup
*vanilla extract	1/2 tsp
*port wine	2 Tbsp
*almond (or canola) oil	1/4 cup
canola oil	5 tsp
*egg whites	6 large
milk, nonfat	1/2 cup
rice, brown, short grain	1 cup
cashews	3/4 cup
sesame seeds	1 tsp
corn starch	3 tsp
*raspberries, frozen	2 1/2 cups
Grand Marnier	3 Tbsp
baby corn, canned	15 oz
chili-garlic paste	1 tsp
fortune cookies	6 regular
rice vinegar	2/3 cup
soy sauce, low sodium	2 Tbsp
nori seaweed, toasted	6 sheets
Japanese soba noodles	15 oz
seitan, canned (braised gluten)	15 oz
asparagus spears	16 medium
avocado	1 large
bell pepper, red	3 medium
berries, fresh	1/2 cup
broccoli	3 cups
cilantro, fresh	1/2 cup
cucumber	1 small
eggplant, Japanese	3 medium
garlic cloves	6 medium
ginger, fresh	4 Tbsp
kale	2 cups
leeks	2 medium
lemons	2 large
mint, fresh	1/4 cup
miso paste	2 1/2 Tbsp
mushrooms, shiitake	2 cups
mushrooms, mixed (shiitake, oyster, morel)	3 cups

onion	1 small
orange rind	2 Tbsp
parsley, fresh	1/4 cup
snow peas	3 cups
tofu, firm	4 oz
won ton wrappers	18 4-inch
*yams	2 medium
cardamom, ground	1/2 tsp
ginger, powdered	1/2 tsp
sea salt	1/2 tsp

vegan option:

chocolate, semi-sweet	4 oz
powdered coffee, instant	1 tsp
orange	1 medium
tofu, silken	12 oz
maple syrup	2/3 cup

Sushi

Passover Meal Shopping List
*delete items if preparing vegan option

port wine	3/4 cup
red wine	1 1/2 cups
mandarin orange slices, canned	22 oz
green olives	1/3 cup
tomatoes, canned or fresh	8 oz
canola oil	1 Tbsp
olive oil, virgin	1/3 cup
*yogurt, nonfat	1 1/4 cups
cherries, dried	1 cup
dates, pitted	1 1/2 cups
peaches or apricots, dried	1 cup
prunes, dried	1 cup
matzo crackers	8 crackers
matzo meal	4 cups
almonds	1/2 cup
walnuts	1/2 cup
apple cider or juice	3 cups
apples	4 medium
beets	4 medium
broccoli	4 cups
cabbage	1 cup
carrots	9 medium
celery stalks	4 medium
chives	1/4 cup
garlic cloves	10 medium
lemons	2 medium
lime	1 medium
mint	1/2 cup
mixed salad greens (green and red leaves)	8 cups
mushrooms	2 cups
onions	3 large
onion, red	1 small
parsley, Italian	2 cups
potatoes, russet	3 medium
spinach, fresh	4 cups
strawberries, fresh	1 cup
honey	1 Tbsp
vegetable stock	3 1/4 cups
caraway seeds	1/4 tsp
cinnamon	1 stick
cloves	3 whole
coriander, ground	1/2 tsp
ginger powder	1/4 tsp
Italian herbs	1 tsp
paprika	1 1/2 Tbsp
pepper, ground	1/2 tsp
sea salt	3 tsp
vinegar, balsamic	1 Tbsp

Easter Brunch Shopping List
*delete items if preparing vegan option

*baking powder	1 tsp
*brown sugar	1 1/4 cups
*confectioner's sugar	1/2 cup
*flour, whole wheat pastry	2 1/2 cups
*vanilla extract	1 tsp
white beans, cooked	15 oz
*pineapple chunks	4 oz
mustard, Dijon	1 tsp
*canola oil	1 Tbsp
canola oil spray	1 can
olive oil, extra virgin	1 Tbsp
olive oil, virgin	1 Tbsp
*egg whites	5 large
*milk, nonfat	1 cup
*cheese, parmesan	1/2 cup
*yogurt, nonfat, plain	3/4 cup
*dried fruit (apricots, prunes)	1 cup
*pecans	1/2 cup
soy sauce, low sodium	1/2 tsp
asparagus spears	24 medium
*carrots	2 medium
carrots with tops	18 small
lemons	2 medium
mushrooms	2 cups
onion	1 medium
oranges	2 medium
orange juice	1/4 cup
parsley	1/2 cup
spinach leaves, fresh	6 oz
squash, baby yellow	12
vegetable stock	1/4 cup
*cinnamon, ground	1 tsp
dill weed	1/2 tsp

*ginger, candied	8 pieces
ginger powder	1 tsp
Italian herbs, dried	1 tsp
sea salt	1 1/2 tsp
vinegar, balsamic	1/4 cup

vegan option:

canola oil (or almond oil)	3 Tbsp
cheese, soy parmesan	1/2 cup
soy milk	1 cup
triple sec liqueur	4 Tbsp
flax seeds	2 Tbsp
grapefruit juice, fresh	3 cups
mint, fresh	1/4 cup

Peppers

Cinco De Mayo Fiesta Shopping list
delete items if preparing vegan option

sugar	1 cup
*sweet, condensed milk, nonfat	14 oz
*vanilla extract	1 tsp
black beans, cooked	15 oz
garbanzo beans, cooked	8 oz
refried beans, nonfat	15 oz
corn, cooked	20 oz
stewed tomatoes	30 oz
almond oil (or canola)	3 Tbsp
olive oil, virgin	2 Tbsp
*cheese, nonfat Monterey jack	1/2 cup
*cheese, low-fat Monterey jack	1 cup
*egg whites	6 large
cointreau or triple sec	1 1/3 cups
tequila, clear	1 cup
corn tortillas	12 medium
pecans	1/4 cup
seitan, canned (oriental foods)	15 oz
soy sauce	1 tsp
avocado	1 medium
bell peppers, red, for roasting	5 large
chiles, poblano	6 medium
cilantro, fresh	1 cup
garlic cloves	9 medium
jicama	1 large
limes	12 large
mint	6 sprigs
orange	1 small
onion	1 1/2 medium
onion	1 small
*raspberries or blueberries, fresh	1 cup
*sweet potato	1 small
tomato salsa	4 oz
tomato	1 large
tomatoes	2 medium
cayenne pepper	1/2 tsp
chile powder	1/4 tsp
cumin, ground	1 3/4 tsp

oregano, dried	2 1/2 tsp
paprika	1/8 tsp
red pepper, crushed	1/2 tsp
sea salt	1/2 tsp
baked tortilla chips	2 cups
tomato sauce	21 oz

vegan option:

rum, dark	2 Tbsp
canola oil	2 Tbsp
soy cheese, Monterey jack flavor	1 cup
banana, ripe	1 large
plantains (or bananas)	3 small
rice milk	2 cups
maple syrup	1/3 cup
cinnamon powder	1/8 teaspoon

Fourth of July Celebration Shopping List

delete items if preparing vegan option

flour, all purpose	3 Tbsp
red wine	2/3 cup
seltzer water	4 cups
bread, whole wheat	1 slice
grape juice	4 cups
granola, less than 30% calories from fat	1 1/2 cups
olive oil, extra virgin	2 1/2 Tbsp
olive oil, virgin	4 1/2 Tbsp
*cheese, nonfat, Mozzarella	8 oz
*cheese, part skim, Mozzarella	8 oz
*milk, nonfat	1/3 cup
*Parmesan cheese	6 Tbsp
*yogurt, nonfat, plain	3 Tbsp
blueberries, frozen	2 cups
strawberries, frozen	2 cups
tapioca, quick cooking	2 Tbsp
almonds, sliced	1/4 cup
soy sauce, low sodium	1 tsp
lasagna noodles, spinach	9 medium

star-shaped noodles	1/4 cup
apples	2 cups
asparagus spears	1 lb
basil, fresh	1/2 cup
berries, mixed, fresh	1/4 cup
bell pepper, red	1 medium
bell pepper, red	1 large
blueberries, fresh	2 1/2 cups
cauliflower	1 medium
cucumber	1 medium
green beans	2 cups
garlic	2 heads
jicama	1 small
lemons	2 medium
lime	1 medium
mint, fresh	1/4 cup
mushrooms	2 cups
onion, white	1 medium
onion, white	1 small
parsley	3 1/4 cups
spinach leaves	9 cups
strawberries, fresh	2 cups
tofu, firm	8 oz
tomatoes	25 medium
cayenne pepper	1/4 tsp
cinnamon, ground	1/4 tsp
cumin seed, ground	1 tsp
dill weed	1 tsp
Italian herbs, dried	1 1/2 tsp
paprika	1 tsp
sea salt	3/4 tsp
maple syrup	1/4 cup
vinegar, Balsamic	6 Tbsp

vegan option:

soy milk	1 cup
tofu, firm	16 oz
oregano, dried	1 tsp

Summer Brunch Shopping List
*delete items if preparing vegan option

flour, all purpose	3/4 cup
flour, whole wheat pastry	1 1/4 cups
sugar	1/2 cup
wine, port	1/3 cup
wine, red	1/2 cup
wine, white	1 cup
sparkling cider	1–2 bottles
hearts of palm	30 oz
mustard, Dijon	3/4 tsp
canola oil	1/2 cup
olive oil, virgin	3 Tbsp
olive oil, extra virgin	2 1/2 Tbsp
*goat cheese	1/3 cup
cheese, Parmesan, or soy	4 Tbsp
rice, arborio	2 cups
tapioca, quick cooking	1/4 cup
soy sauce, low-sodium	1 1/2 tsp
apples, for baking	3 medium
basil, fresh	3/4 cup
blueberries, fresh	2 cups
garlic cloves	7 medium
leeks	2 medium
lemon	1/2 medium
lime	1 medium
edible flowers (if available)	12 medium
mushrooms, wild (a mixture)	8 cups
onion	1 medium
parsley, fresh	1/2 cup
plums	10 small
salad greens, mixed	8 cups
scallions	3 medium
tomatoes	10 medium
tomatoes, cherry	18 medium
vegetable stock	6 cups
cinnamon powder	1/8 tsp
dill weed	1/2 tsp
ginger, candied	2 Tbsp
ginger powder	1/4 tsp
Italian herbs, dried	1 tsp
pepper, black, ground	1/2 tsp
sea salt	1 tsp
tomato sauce	1 cup
vinegar, Balsamic	6 Tbsp

Fall Equinox Party Shopping List
*delete items if preparing vegan option

flour, all purpose	3/4 cup
flour, whole wheat pastry	1 cup
sugar	1/4 tsp
wine, white	1/4 cup
garbanzo beans, cooked	15 oz
pumpkin purée, cooked	15 oz
canola oil	1/2 cup
olive oil, extra virgin	2 tsp
olive oil, virgin	2 Tbsp
*egg whites	4 large
*milk, nonfat	3 cups
nonfat whipped topping, pressurized	1 can
cornmeal, coarse	2 cups
soy sauce, low-sodium	1 tsp
basil	1/4 cup
beets	3 medium
bell pepper, red	1 medium
carrots	2 medium
fennel	1 1/2 cups
garlic cloves	5 medium
ginger, fresh	1 Tbsp
green beans	2 cups
herbs, fresh	1/2 cup
leek	1 medium
lemon	1 medium
mushrooms, shiitake	1 cup
onions	2 medium
parsley	3/4 cup
raspberries, fresh or frozen	1/2 cup
salad greens, mixed	10 cups
squash, butternut	1 medium
squash, yellow, baby if possible	2 cups
vegetable stock	1 1/4 cups
cinnamon powder	1 1/8 tsp
cloves, ground	1/4 tsp
cumin powder	1/4 tsp
curry powder	1/2 tsp

ginger, candied	1 Tbsp
Italian herbs	2 1/2 tsp
sea salt	3 1/2 tsp
maple syrup	1 cup
vinegar, Balsamic	2 Tbsp

Birthday Dinner Party Shopping List
delete items if preparing vegan option

baking powder	2 tsp
baking soda	2 1/2 tsp
chocolate, semi-sweet	8 1/4 oz
cocoa powder	1/2 cup
flour, all purpose	1 cup
flour, whole wheat pastry	1 cup
sugar	1 2/3 cups
vanilla extract	1 1/2 Tbsp
wine, port	1/2 cup
wine, red	1/2 cup
wine, white	1 cup
bread crumbs, whole wheat	1 cup
pita bread, whole wheat	3 rounds
artichoke hearts, in water, cooked	15 oz
coffee, espresso (brewed)	1/4 cup
capers	2 Tbsp
canola oil	1/3 cup
olive oil, extra virgin	4 Tbsp
olive oil, virgin	1 Tbsp
*cheese, nonfat mozzarella	1/2 cup
*cheese, Parmesan	1/4 cup
*egg whites	14 large
*milk, nonfat	1 cup
soy milk	1 1/2 cups
fillo dough (frozen pastries)	12 sheets
cherries, frozen	2 cups
rum, dark	4 Tbsp
almond slices	1 Tbsp
hazelnuts	3 Tbsp
pecans	3 oz
basil, fresh	1/2 cup

bell peppers, red, for roasting	3 large
broccoli	4 cups
carrots	2 medium
cherries, fresh	1/2 cup
garlic cloves	13 medium
leeks	3 medium
lemon	1 medium
miso paste	2 tsp
mushrooms	6 cups
mushrooms, wild	1 cup
mushrooms, shiitake	1 1/2 cups
onions	2 medium
parsley, fresh	3/4 cup
potatoes, russet	4 medium
yams	2 cups
soy sauce, low-sodium	1 tsp
vegetable stock	1 cup
pepper, ground	1/2 tsp
sea salt	2 1/2 tsp

vegan option:

soy mozzarella, grated	1/2 cup
soy milk	1 cup
tofu, firm	6 oz

Mushrooms

148

INDEX

About the Author

I am a family physician, husband, and the father of two young boys, ages seven and ten. My passion is teaching people to create delicious, healthy, and easy-to-make meals. Day to day, my work focuses upon researching nutrition and longevity, promoting wellness in my community, and teaching physicians specializing in family medicine.

As a physician, I have observed that food plays a critical role in our well-being. Years ago, I realized that food choices influenced my patients' long-term health far more than the prescriptions I wrote for them. More recently, I've discovered that food choices influence how we feel from moment to moment, not just over the years.

As in many vegetarian homes, my family and I enjoy excellent health and increased energy because of the nutrient-rich plant foods that we add to our diet. Also, we prosper in the knowledge that choosing a plant-based diet benefits the earth's environment, too.

My wife, Nicole, and I have been fortunate to work as volunteers in medical facilities in over a dozen countries. These cultural experiences have greatly influenced our cooking and introduced us to a variety of ethnic flavors and ideas.

Nicole and I spend most holidays in our own home, inviting family and friends to join us. For these special occasions, we like to create meals that combine artistry, flavor, and a sense of tradition.

For twenty years, I have researched cooking, nutrition, food, exercise, and their combined impact on health and vitality. I've reviewed thousands of medical articles over the past years to ensure that the ingredients in my recipes promote good health. My goal has been to combine cutting-edge nutritional advances with mouthwatering, vitamin-rich, low-fat recipes.

Vegetarian Holiday Feasts takes a step beyond the detailed nutrition information in my first book, *The 28-Day Antioxidant Diet Program.* In this book, I'll share twenty years of vegetarian cooking to make these recipes your tastiest and healthiest holiday feasts ever.

For vitality tips, my lecture schedule, or to see my recipe of the month—visit my web site at:
www.drmasley.com